A Mysterious Mantle

A Mysterious Mantle

The Biography of Hulda Niebuhr

Elizabeth Caldwell

The Pilgrim Press
Cleveland, Ohio

To my family
with thanks and love

The Pilgrim Press, Cleveland, Ohio 44115
© 1992 by The Pilgrim Press

Cover photo and photos in chapters 4 and 5 courtesy of the archives of Jesuit-Krauss-McCormick Library, McCormick Theological Seminary, Chicago. Photos in chapters 1, 2, and 3 courtesy of Carol Niebuhr Buchanan.

Cover design by Cindy Dolan
Book design by EastWord Publications Development

Printed in the United States of America
The paper used in this publication is acid free and meets the minimum requirements of American National Standard for Information Sciences-Permanence of Paper for Printed Library Materials, ANSI Z39.48–1984

97 96 95 94 93 92   5 4 3 2 1

Library of Congress Cataloging-in-Publication Data

Caldwell, Elizabeth, 1948–
    A mysterious mantle : the biography of Hulda Niebuhr / Elizabeth
Caldwell.
        p. cm.
    Includes bibliographical references.
    ISBN 0-8298-0923-6 (alk. paper)
    1. Niebuhr, Hulda. 1889–1959. 2. Christian educators—United
States—Biography. I. Title.
BV1470.3.N45C35   1992
268'.092—dc20
    [B]   92–26567
                                                             CIP

Contents

Foreword

In 1924 Hulda Niebuhr was gaining a master of arts degree at Boston University, preparing herself academically to become a pioneer woman religious educator in churches and higher education. Boston University recently had graduated another "female first," Georgia Harkness, who would later be recognized as the first woman theologian to teach in Protestant seminaries in the United States. In the fall of 1924 Harkness returned from an American seminar in Europe, where the group gained firsthand contact with the devastation wrought throughout the continent by World War I.

Writing to Edgar Brightman, Borden Parker Bowne Professor of Philosophy at Boston University, Harkness shared her excitement and told him of some of "our leading lights" who were on the trip. One was the young Reinhold Niebuhr, then pastor of Bethel evangelical Church in Detroit. But Brightman would know the name of Reinhold Niebuhr, Harkness continued, because he was the brother of Hulda Niebuhr!

I laughed out loud in the otherwise quiet reading room of the Mugar Library Archives at Boston University when I read Harkness's words in the Brightman Papers on file there. This was probably the only time in his life that Reinhold gained his identity because of his relationship with Hulda Niebuhr. For Reinhold and his brother Helmut Richard bore the family mantle of public repute. Certainly "the brothers Niebuhr" are among the most distinguished scholars of the church and theological academy of the modern day.

I experienced something of the mysterious mantle bequeathed by Gustav and Lydia Niebuhr to their children when I was a student in the master of religious education program at Yale Divinity School in the late 1950s. My courses taken with H. Richard Niebuhr are treasured experiences remembered with gratitude even today. If the top of one's head may be termed a mantle, he rubbed his bald, groping everyday in class to convey the paradoxes of the Christian faith as he so faithfully experienced them.

H. Richard Niebuhr wore loosely the vestment of his distinction as a theological scholar and educator. He was not overly impressed with himself. But in academic circles of higher education, he was known as "the theologian's theologian." Richard and Reinhold were certainly among the most creative thinkers of the generation of neoorthodox theologians and ethicists of the mid-twentieth century.

In the late twentieth century, as feminist scholars unearth the treasures of their female forebears, Elizabeth Caldwell has recovered the lost mantle of Hulda Niebuhr. While the mantles of Reinhold and Richard are obvious and well known by public standards, Hulda's is not readily identifiable, and few people even know her name yet.

In the early years of the century, when most professionals in the field were men, Hulda Niebuhr became a "first female religious educator." She served as associate director of religious education for almost twenty years, from 1930 until 1946, at one of the largest and most active Protestant churches in the United States, Madison Avenue Presbyterian Church in New York City. Over those many years, the position of director was held always by a man.

Then Hulda Niebuhr joined the faculties of the Presbyterian College of Christian Education and McCormick Theological seminary in Chicago for another lengthy stint from 1945 until 1959. McCormick initially offered her the position of instructor, even though she had previously served as assistant professor of religious education at Boston University and lecturer in the field at New York University. After negotiation, she came onto the faculty as an associate professor. Active to the end, Hulda died in the doctor's office when she went for a checkup during the spring of her planned retirement.

Hulda Niebuhr fashioned her own mantle as a female professional religious educator, walking a treacherous career course within the institutions of family, church, and higher education. Elizabeth Caldwell tells that story with passion, reason, and persuasion. Currently holding Niebuhr's former position as professor in the field of religious education at McCormick Seminary, Caldwell is recovering the mantle of a self-chosen mother of her own. The complexity of Hulda Niebuhr's vocational journey, and of the mysterious mantle that she bore, unfolds under this sensitively rendered account. And Hulda's story embodies the hidden greatness of countless foremothers in the sacred and secular world.

Richard Reinhold Niebuhr, son of H. Richard Niebuhr and nephew of Hulda and Reinhold, recognized that his aunt wore the "mysterious mantle" of a theological educator and social pioneer, bequeathed by the parents to the children, as much as did her brothers. Hulda's nephew particularly noted the inheritance that she gained from her father, a major public leader in the German Evangelical Church Society of the West at the turn of the century.

Elizabeth Caldwell discerns that Hulda's mysterious mantle was as much an inheritance from her mother as from her father. Indeed, her gifts as a professional educator were more the direct legacy of female than male experience and characteristics. In 1931, Hulda wrote a book entitled *Greatness Passing By*, a collection of stories exemplifying models of faithful witness to the Christian life. The biography presents the greatness of Hulda Niebuhr and passes it on to us as her legacy of *how* to teach, her methodology of being an effective Christian educator in the home, seminary, and church.

In the late twentieth century, theological educators increasingly recognize the truth that *how* to teach, not just *what* to teach, must be at the forefront of their purpose and work. Strong lectures will continue to be a primary means of communicating the faith in various educational settings. However, we are realizing finally that for the faith to be internalized in the experience of individuals and communities, "educated faithful companionship" must characterize the model of Christian leadership as much as proclamation of the word from pulpit and platform.

Hulda bequeaths to laity and clergy of the church in the late twentieth century the mysterious mantle of how to communicate the faith in word and action, both in formal and informal educational settings. The Christian faith becomes transformative only as we are moved by the *presence* of living ordinary saints, not just by their words.

Our loss is that Hulda Niebuhr did not write the magnum opus, her theory of religious education, so that we could study the theory and practice of how to teach—and how to live—from such an authority. However, we gain today through Elizabeth Caldwell's insightful account of Niebuhr's life and thought.

Through the involving story of Hulda's vocational journey, her own example of educated faithful companionship, with her family, students, colleagues, and friends, unfolds in her private and public experiences. Hulda Niebuhr was not a feminist, but she was of the generation of prefeminist mothers in the faith who opened doors of opportunity and equality with men in church and society.

I invite you to venture forth with me on a vocational journey with Hulda Niebuhr and Elizabeth Caldwell. And may our lives as Christian educators, both personally and professionally, be changed in the process, just as theirs were.

ROSEMARY SKINNER KELLER
Professor of Religion and American Culture
Garrett-Evangelical Theological Seminary

Acknowledgments

Recovering the story and voice of Hulda Niebuhr began as a paper for a graduate course. The evolvement of this paper into a dissertation and finally into a book represents the contribution of many persons whose individual memories and stories have played an essential role in reweaving Hulda Niebuhr's life and work into the history of the Niebuhr family, the field of religious education, and the educational and religious leadership of women in the United States in the twentieth century.

Members of the Niebuhr family—Ursula Niebuhr, Christopher Niebuhr, Carol Buchanan, and Richard R. Niebuhr—provided important help with sources and confirmation of biographical details.

Students of Hulda Niebuhr at McCormick Theological Seminary generously shared their memories of classes, course syllabi, and reading lists, thus providing rich sources for reconstructing her philosophy of religious education. Faculty colleagues of Hulda Niebuhr and spouses of faculty members at McCormick Theological Seminary were another important source in collecting the story of her life and teaching on the McCormick campus.

Rosemary Keller's insightful wisdom and patient guidance in helping me to bring this quiet woman into voice is greatly appreciated. My work and dialog with her and her faculty colleagues—Dorothy Jean Furnish, Jack Seymour, and Jim Ashbrook—at Garrett Evangelical Theological Seminary and with Josef Barton at Northwestern University were essential in the articulation of research questions and conceptual categories important to the development and writing of this biography.

The research and writing of this biography were completed while serving on the faculty at McCormick Theological Seminary in Chicago. A grant to McCormick Theological Seminary from the Lilly Endowment supported my research. I am appreciative of Robert Lynn's commitment to the history and vision for the future of the field of religious education. I am grateful to the administration of McCormick—David Ramage, president, and Robert Worley, dean of the faculty—for their help and for the time made available to me to complete this work. My colleagues on the faculty have continually supported me both by asking probing, critical questions and by expressing encouragement and support. Thanks also go to Doran Hill, faculty secretary, for his patient help with many drafts of the manuscript.

I am grateful for my friend and editor, Barbara Withers, who had the vision for the telling of the story of this important woman in our history.

Finally I wish to thank my family, whose voices of support and guidance have sustained me and who have provided insights into understanding the importance of the activities of being and doing in the person of the teacher. For the mantles they possess and pass on and for their presence in my life I am thankful.

Clara Augusta Hulda Niebuhr as a young woman, c. 1904

Introduction

THE LAST DECADE OF THE TWENTIETH CENTURY provides a lens through which to examine, remember, and celebrate advances made in the dismantling of separate spheres for women in American culture. Denied the vote, equal educational opportunities, careers, jobs with renumeration equal to that of males, and denied voice in decision making within the society, women have worked to claim a place in a world in which they have not been viewed as legitimate heirs.

Finally in these last years of the twentieth century, mantles of leadership, education, and vocation are being passed to both females and males. The examination of the life of one woman, Clara Augusta Hulda Niebuhr, whose life bridged the changing world of women's roles within the family and culture, demonstrates in concrete ways the evolving process of gender free mantles. Such a process, which is far from complete, is empowered by the example of this woman's life, which was lived in contrast to the career limitations made explicit by her family and culture.

In his forward to William Chrystal's biography of Gustav Niebuhr, Richard Reinhold Niebuhr, the son of H. Richard and Florence Niebuhr and nephew of Hulda Niebuhr, reflected on the title of the book, *A Father's Mantle*. Considering his family members, "the cloud of witnesses" who led the way, Niebuhr alluded to the complexities that are present within families.

> How all these near ancestors strengthened and shaped one another, while also sometimes disagreeing with one another, is knowledge of which I have only intimations, and do not expect ever to possess it, but the suspicion lingers that family legacies while they can be intricately woven and become deeply cherished "garments", are woven out of many lives and are of a different order from prophetic mantles.[1]

One of the benefits of Chrystal's work that Niebuhr most appreciated was the chance to gain

> a still deeper admiration for the innovative and imaginative Hulda, my aunt; and if in some degree she inherited her fortitude and great abilities as an educator from the father who so strongly disapproved of her aspirations to an education, then it may be she as much as any other to whom a mysterious "mantle" fell.[2]

Some value her contribution as the author of stories for children and as a leader in the field of religious education. To students, she is remembered as Miss Niebuhr, professor of religious education at McCormick Theological Seminary from 1946 to 1959, one who "discerned the weakness and limitations of her students but whose friendship and appreciation of their possibilities opened up to them the way of growth and Christian usefulness."[3]

Her obituary noted that she was the sister of famed theologians Reinhold and H. Richard Niebuhr. To the children on the McCormick campus, she was the daughter of Mrs. Lydia Niebuhr who loved to entertain children on the campus and in the neighborhood with creative art activities and community parades. Colleagues and friends of Hulda remember her as a gracious lady who with her mother made their home a "bright center of Christian love and friendship to children, students, faculty, and alumni."[4]

At first glance at the life of Clara Augusta Hulda Niebuhr, one might conclude, as has Helen Haroutunian, one of her neighbors on the McCormick campus, that "most of what she gave is invisible."[5] Hulda was not world famous as her brothers. She was probably less well known by many of the children living on the McCormick campus than was her mother. Hulda went about her life and her profession in very quiet ways, passing on her faith, her love of teaching, and her commitment to learning. These are qualities that can not be measured or counted. So perhaps Helen Haroutunian is correct. If so, many people today still carry with them Hulda Niebuhr's invisible gifts.

American culture has been gifted by the contribution of theological leadership made by the Niebuhrs in the twentieth century. Weaving this particular women, in this particular family, back into the "fabric of culture" is essential in developing a complete picture of the contribution of the Niebuhrs.[6] Such weaving provides evidence for Richard R. Niebuhr's significant suggestion that Hulda, not her brothers, was the inheritor of the mysterious family "mantle".

Biographers, in writing about their art, discuss the passion, the feeling that must be present in writing about a persons's life. Blance Wiesen Cook suggests that such passion seeks to "redress the wrongs, reconstitute the spirit, restore and celebrate the subject."[7] I have been drawn to the person of Hulda Niebuhr for precisely those reasons. As a religious educator working with congregations and as a professor in a theological institution, the one in which Hulda Niebuhr lived and worked for fifteen years, I seek to "redress the wrongs" that have prohibited Hulda's voice from being heard as an educational pioneer and transforming leader within McCormick Theological Seminary.

When speaking with Hulda's former students, the spirit of her being, her vision and her faith, are articulated as frequently as her pedagogy and philosophy. This biography seeks to reconstitute Hulda's spirit and to begin to define a feminist educational perspective in terms of pedagogy, style or presence, and institutional relationships.

During her career as an educator, Hulda studied, worked, and taught in six institutions. An examination of her relationship with these two congregations and four educational institutions indicates cultural attitudes and expectations in relation to gender roles, issues of authority, and styles of leadership. Understanding her in the context of these institutions as she worked our her relationship to her family and discovered the power of her own voice is essential in identifying the ways in which she used her own resources for her continued individuation and maturation.

I am drawn to this subject because, if we are to begin to understand the Niebuhrs as a family, we must restore the women—the oldest child and only daughter, Hulda, and the wife and mother, Lydia—back into their places in the family portrait, where they have been virtually invisible until this time. Even more invisible is Hulda's place in the portrait of leaders in the field of religious education. Such restorations thus enable the long-overdue celebration of Hulda Niebuhr's life and work. This biography seeks to develop a complete photograph of Hulda Niebuhr, working intentionally to let her voice speak through her relationships with family, friends and colleagues, her writing, her teaching and her leadership within the insitutions with which she was associated.

Richard R. Niebuhr has suggested that when considering the members of the Niebuhr family and the legacies which were woven from their family garments, it is possible to conclude that Hulda inherited a "mysterious mantle." An obvious mantle that she received was her gift as a teacher, but this was a gift that was also shared by two of her brothers. The question remains, what was mysterious about the mantle she inherited?

Hulda was raised in a home that modeled faithful Christian community. Her parents provided the kind of environment that encouraged and supported an educated mind and a faithful Christian spirit. She learned about education and teaching from her experiences in her family and in her church. She learned about faithful Christian living from growing up in a family of pastors.

The "woven garment" passed on to her as a mantle was one of educated faithful companionship. She certainly can be described as an educator, one whose work was deeply rooted in faith and her commitment to the church in its mission in the world. In her relationship with church members, with students and with colleagues, Hulda also helped to define the role of a faithful companion. Her teaching went beyond the classroom, beyond the walls of church, lovingly and faithfully shared as friend and pastor with those around her.

The "mysterious mantle" that Hulda inherited—educated faithful companionship—serves as a model for those who seek to understand the relationship between belief and vocation, and between theory and practice. The opportunity to understand the process of her development and individuation and her intentional commitment to the role of teacher make the naming of her mantle less mysterious and more descriptive. Her mantle is significant today in continued reflection on the role of women within the family, the church, educational institutions, and the culture.

Clockwise from top: Walter, Hulda, Helmut Richard, and Reinhold Niebuhr

"Warm Little Frictions" (1889–1918)

HIGH SCHOOL GRADUATION IN 1906 was not an occasion that offered a variety of life choices for Hulda Niebuhr. She completed her course work with honors, yet continued to live at home obediently obeying her father's wishes and following the model of her mother as a volunteer leader in the church. Instead of opening up possibilities for vocational choice, this important time in Hulda's life was limited by the roles available to women in the culture, the traditions of her German immigrant family, and the Evangelical church in which her family had a long history of leadership. The fact that Hulda was able to move beyond these limitations is a credit to her convictions and personal vision for her vocational journey.

NIEBUHR FAMILY TRADITION

Hulda Niebuhr was born on March 9, 1889, in San Francisco, California, the first child and only daughter of Gustav Niebuhr and Lydia Hosto Niebuhr. Gustav had immigrated from Germany in 1881 at age 18, and while working on the farm of a cousin in Illinois, he found his vocation and identity in the Salem church, which belonged to the German Evangelical Church Society of the West. This represented a religious tradition consistent with the one in which he had been confirmed as a child in Germany.[1]

After completing studies at Eden Theological Seminary near St. Louis, Gustav was ordained in 1885 and moved to San Francisco to work with new arrivals from Germany, helping the synod's missionary in the Far West, Edward Hosto. Working as Hosto's assistant in the establishment of church colonies in the San Francisco area was his daughter Lydia.

When the Niebuhr and Hosto families were joined by the marriage of Gustav and Lydia in 1887, religious traditions were brought into the union. For both Lydia and Gustav, religious education in the home and the church had been of great importance. Together they sought to form their family and the culture in ways consistent with their faith.

Ideological struggles were taking place in San Francisco that represented signs of the changing values in society. It was a "Gilded Age" (1850-1900), characterized by the emergence of an upper-class elite, strong economic growth, and the development of a capitalist ideology. Herbert Gutman has identified two ideas that sanctioned this concept of industrial laissez faire.

The first idea was that no relationship was perceived between economic activity in the business world and a moral ethic. As the importance of traditional religious sanctions declined, the importance of secular values and institutions increased. Second, Protestant churches reinforced the secular business ethic by preaching and teaching a theology that equated being poor and unsuccessful with being sinful. Wealth and success were identified with God's grace.[2] A few Protestant clergy promoted a different theology, the Social Gospel. They were in the minority in the face of Gilded Age Protestantism, which was "viewed as a conformist, 'culture bound' Christianity that warmly embraced the rising industrialist, drained the aspiring rich of conscience, and confused or pacified the poor."[3]

Edward Hosto and his family, including Gustav Niebuhr, were leading clergy in the Evangelical Synod in California, working to preach and teach a theology different from that which they found in that context. Reports to the denomination highlighted the difficulty of starting churches because of the indifference of the people. An early German pastor, Frederick Fox, gave his assessment of the difficulty of this particular mission field.

The chief and all-prevailing evil among us is undoubtedly the sinful love of money. Almost everyone who came here in early days came for gold, and it is astonishing to notice how readily later immigrants, cousins and nephews of these "old Californians," bow at the shrine of the "Golden Calf" with abject devotion, at the sacrifice of early religious training, sacred principles, and alas, genuine faith in the redeemer of the world. This preponderating love for the almighty dollar leaves little, if any, room for the comforting love of God in Christ.[4]

The roots of both the Hostos and the Niebuhrs, grounding these families in faithful and ethical Christian living, were planted deep in their early religious formation. As adults, Gustav and Lydia must have been confused by the conformist Christianity of the Gilded Age yet determined to hold out another alternative. Their confusion also included amazement that Christians could forget their identity and calling. They were never confused, however, about their own values, goals, and ministry. What they saw and heard confirmed their vocation and became an impetus for their work, both in the church and in the formation of their family.

The theology that was foundational to Gustav's practice of ministry and the one that he sought to infuse in his children is illustrated in one of his sermonic essays: "We are truly Evangelical so long as we hear the voice of the Good Shepherd and walk in his footsteps."[5]

Evangelical was defined for Gustav in the conception of faith as a personal experience with God, with the expectation that it would be acted out in daily life. Such a faith was based on an understanding of the Bible as God's Word. Evangelical Christian faith, for Gustav, also implied a commitment to church union. These were the essential tenets of his theology that he sought to teach, preach, and pass on to his children.[6]

Jon Diefenthaler has described the Niebuhr family as one that "seems to have supplied both incentive for scholarly pursuits and a setting that nurtured a deep, personal devotion to Christianity. Among its members, piety and intellect were never incompatible."[7] The blending of the German tradition with that of an evangelical theological tradition produced a denomination committed to education for persons of all ages, an ecumenical church consciousness, a social concern for the ill and handicapped in society, and a zealous piety. The impact of the German culture and the Evangelical Synod on this family accounts for many factors inherent in their development and formation as individuals and as family members.

Biographers of the Niebuhr men have noted the important place of the home in shaping the children.[8] Hulda, the oldest child and only daughter, was also greatly affected by her home life and the complementary parental models of Gustav and Lydia.

To understand the social conditioning of the Niebuhr children, one must visualize the collaborative style of parenting of Lydia and Gustav. Chrystal has suggested that Gustav's "ideas provided a significant starting point for his children," and that "his model was far more important for the intellectual development of his children" than was Lydia's.[9] Such statements perpetuate a gender specific and "separate spheres" approach to understanding parental training that assumes a hierarchy of learning models. It also diminishes the important educational opportunities provided by the mother. A clue to understanding the social conditioning of the children is found by visualizing a collaborative style exhibited by Lydia and Gustav.

Hulda's journey within the family provided her with deep roots in a loving family, a lifelong commitment to education, an understanding of people and the depths of human need, and a faith in God that sustained her daily life and work. Even more than a secular education, her parents wanted her to have a life lived in faithful response to God. Unlike other "democratic families" in the late nineteenth century and probably more similar to immigrant family tradition, Hulda's parents passed on to her the mantle of a Christian faith tradition.

Her life was an example of the intricate weaving of family legacies. The mysterious mantle that fell to Hulda was the combination of a family and a faith tradition that nourished and sustained her as she moved into her vocation as an educated professional woman in the twentieth century.

IN THE FOOTSTEPS OF HER MOTHER

Biographers of the Niebuhr men have described Lydia in varying terms. For William Chrystal she was "a striking woman who stood out in many ways...deeply spiritual...an indispensable part of Gustav's ministry."[10] James Fowler described her as a "woman of great character and ability."[11] June Bingham's portrait of Lydia emphasized her energy and magnetic personality. In describing the Niebuhr household, which often included both invited and drop-in guests, Bingham said, "Fortunately, Lydia Niebuhr had so much energy, so much laughter, so much expertness in cooking, sewing, and toy-making, that her large and unpredictable household did not overpower her."[12]

She lacked formal schooling, Richard Fox notes in commenting on the help Lydia gave as organist and Sunday school assistant in her father's church, "but ran her parish tasks with discipline and enthusiasm. Like her husband, she reveled in work."[13]

The *St. Louis Post-Dispatch* highlighted her "unofficial role" as "Associate Pastor" when she received an honorary degree from Lindenwood College in 1953. "She herself has never held a title, but to members of the family she's known as the 'Associate Pastor.'"[14] In presenting Lydia

Niebuhr the degree, the president of Lindenwood's board of directors stated:

> In days past, Lindenwood College has honored men and women for a
> variety of worthy reasons: some for their erudition, some for their
> statesmanship, some for their scientific knowledge, some for their
> public service, some for their nobel churchmanship and some for their
> business brilliance. Today we honor one who is unfamed in any of
> these spheres, but has achieved unique distinction in the spheres upon
> the quality of which learning, statesmanship, science, public service,
> churchmanship, and business brilliance are primarily dependent:
> motherhood and home.[15]

In contrast to defining her in terms of what she didn't do or have, Chrystal
described Lydia as an equal partner with her husband, not his assistant.
"Together Gustav and Lydia founded the first synod church on the Pacific
Coast, St. John's in San Francisco, where they met considerable resistance."[16] While they labored together to give this congregation a good
beginning, Lydia also gave birth to two other children: Walter and Herbert,
who died in infancy.

In 1891, the Niebuhrs moved to Wright City, Missouri, where Gustav had
received a call from the Board for Home Missions of the Evangelical Synod
to be involved in the organization of new parishes and welfare homes. It was
there that Reinhold and Helmut Richard were born. Fox's conclusion is
most likely correct that the children did not see much of their father during
those ten years. A large part of the day-to-day parenting must have been the
responsibility of Lydia. She expressed a democratic approach to the rearing
of children. When interviewed much later in life, Lydia made these
revealing comments about her views on raising children.

> They were never made to feel that because they were the preacher's
> children, they were terribly restricted in their activities. . . . I think
> that's a big mistake. I remember when someone doubted if they would
> be permitted to go to the theatre. Why, as long as it was good and
> decent and wholesome entertainment, why shouldn't they go?[17]

When recalling with her daughter, Hulda, some of the activities she had
made available, including a clubhouse for the boys, Lydia said:

> Yes, we tried to keep the children's activities centered in the home. We
> wanted them to have their friends there and to love their home. But
> they all had chores to do. I think children are happier when they have
> a real part in maintaining the home and a say-so about it. It's good for
> them.[18]

In the Niebuhr home, children were allowed and encouraged to be children.

Ralph Abele, one of Reinhold's assistants at Bethel Evangelical Church, compared the Niebuhr family with Hulda's definitions. In the introduction to her book of stories for children, Hulda defined a teacher's job as effecting for the learners "some usable simplification of the great mass of mankind's experience."[19] Abele applied her definition of a teacher's job to the family.

> "Seminary" means seed-bed, and the world's most famous seed-bed of dedicated souls is the Christian home, especially one presided over by parents with discerning minds supported by abundant physical vitality. The Niebuhr household was a seminary where a child acquired a "usable simplification of the great mass of mankind's experience" and where he was under the nurture of "visible forms of individual saintliness and communal authority."[20]

The family as a seedbed is an apt description of the kind of life that enabled the formation and individuation of Hulda Niebuhr.

VALUES OF THE NIEBUHR FAMILY

Certain values were important in the formation of this family, values that became the foundation for Hulda Niebuhr's own development and the basis for her philosophy of teaching. Seven concepts that provide clues to understanding Niebuhr family life emerge from primary source materials and from biographies of the Niebuhr men.

1 Religious training was a daily event in the Niebuhr home. Devotions, prayers at meals, participation in church life were all norms for each family member. Confirmation training was important for the children just as it had been for their parents.
2 Faithful living was communicated as much by example as by explicit teaching. When drifters would knock at the door asking for a meal, they were taken in. "Gustav Niebuhr said he would never refuse a hungry man a meal or a weary man a bed, and he never did."[21]
3 The home provided a creative learning environment lovingly planned and nurtured by Lydia Niebuhr. Reinhold has said that his mother was a prime factor in the development of his imagination:

> She knew how to set up children's games that sparked activity. She gave them ropes and mattresses for the buggy shed and they trans-formed it into one arena after another: a circus, a World's Fair, a Chautauqua. They mounted their own theatrical skits: Walter and

Reinhold conferred on the plot; Hulda, Helmut [Richard], and other neighborhood kids took their assigned roles.[22]

4 Their home appears to have been one of love and care. Obviously in this household children were accepted for who they were and loved for their individual abilities and gifts.
5 Learning was a priority and the children were expected to attend school and succeed in their studies.
6 Though the children were given great freedom to express themselves, they were not forced to live above others as sometimes happens with "children of the manse."
7 The Niebuhr children also lived with expectations and assumptions about their participation in the family. Chores were assigned and the children were expected to do their share of the work.

HULDA NIEBUHR'S FORMATION IN THE FAMILY

The family culture that provided a loving and faithful household, imaginative play, and intellectual challenge for Hulda at the same time made clear the educational and vocational restraints with which she was to live. The educational expectations and freedoms offered to her brothers were denied to her.

The sociology of gender observable in American culture is the result of years of intentional practice to maintain separate and unequal roles for women and men. Hulda was not allowed by her father to attend college, though he strongly encouraged higher education for her three brothers. In 1959, at the request of June Bingham, Hulda read a draft of Bingham's biography of Reinhold. Hulda took issue with the statement regarding her education and attempted to correct the assumption that her father had denied her an education.

> Even if Reinie tells this story about my education or delayed education, it is here much too simplified to be true to fact. It sounds as if I had to wait for my father's death to get schooling. I attended Lincoln College in his time for courses. My professional career I'm said "to have always wanted" was slow coming into picture. If my aim had been what it sounds like here, I might have achieved it sooner. College was not as generally assumed for both boys and girls in those days as a few decades later. I was very fully occupied.[23]

It is difficult to know how to weigh the evidence between Gustav's adamant stance advocating the role of women in the family and Hulda's experience with him as she pursued a college education. "And in regard to his only daughter, it simply never occurred to Pastor Niebuhr that a girl might be interested in the kind of professional training he was planning for the boys."[24] Hulda's aunt, Sister Adele Hosto, provided another role model, that of a single woman serving the church as a parish deaconess, a career option for women that Gustav advocated.

Gustav was very outspoken in his views on women's education. It was not an issue of women being less intelligent than men. Rather, he saw women's reaching for higher education, particularly a scientific education, as a desire for emancipation. But he did not see emancipation as a wholesome goal. "What the emancipated woman really desires is neither scientific nor spiritual development, but rather enjoyment, respect, freedom, and sport, together with freedom from all the burdensome duties and responsibilities. For the taproot of all emancipation is egoism."[25]

Gustav believed that such emancipation would prevent his daughter from being a good "marriage prospect for an educated younger man."[26] In Gustav's thinking, education led to emancipation and such freedom was not a quality desired by a man for his wife. The implication is that Hulda's education was to prepare her for one thing—to be a wife and mother. Any other life or calling would surely lead her to a life of impoverishment of heart, spirit, and soul.[27]

It is essential to reflect on Gustav's writings about the emancipated woman in relation to the reality of his experience and to the historical context. Lydia's partnership with him in establishing churches in the Evangelical Synod and her supervision and maintenance of the household during Gustav's absences cannot be described as a life lived totally dependent on her husband. And Lydia is remembered as one possessing great organizational skill, an indispensable help in ministry.[28] No doubt her experience as "parish assistant" with her father, her husband, and her son Reinhold qualified Lydia for that description.

Gustav seems to have equated emancipation with the condition of a woman who had freedom of choice about her life, her education, her vocation, her marital status. So perhaps his resistance to Hulda continuing her education was a fear of the freedom or freedoms she might choose. Hulda graduated with honors from Lincoln High School in 1906 but continued to live at home obediently obeying her father's wishes and following the model of her mother.

Whatever Hulda's own wishes, she remained at home after graduation and took on a succession of parish tasks: teacher in the parochial school, instructor in the Sunday School, vice-president of the Young

People's Society, organist and member of the mixed choir. She was a mirror image of her mother, who was also an organist, secretary of the Ladies' Society, superintendent of the Home Visitation Department, and member of the administrative board of the Deaconess Hospital.[29]

Gustav's German family tradition probably encountered one of its greatest cultural shocks when he was confronted by the appearance of women demanding equality in every place in society. When Hulda finished high school in 1906, the women's movement had made great strides in dismantling separate spheres for women. Education, employment, and the diversification of home and family relationships were signs of the increasing changes in women's lives. "The growing frequency of women's new experiences in public organizations and occupational life marked one of the ways in which the outlines of twentieth-century America were already taking shape."[30]

At a time when Gustav Niebuhr was equating emancipation with egoism, the women's movement contended that selfhood, self-discovery, and claiming a voice were essential to emancipation. Nancy Cott identified three arenas of effort in the women's movement in the nineteenth century, arenas that provided a basis for future development for women in the twentieth century. One of the earliest ways that women began to move out of silence in the home to activity in the world was in the area of service and social action. The church oftentimes provided an outlet for women to gain "new strength in collectivity and forms for self-assertion."[31] Gustav, as will be shown later in his advocacy and support of the deaconess movement, would have had no problem with this area of women's work.

A second arena involved the active campaign for women's rights, the fight for equality in the legal, political, economic, and civic arenas of society. This probably would have been an example for Gustav of women's growing egoism. For Gustav, it was proper, useful, and beneficial for women to give of themselves to others. That was the role he believed they were to fulfill in life; but for women to speak out in their own behalf, to assert their voice, to demand equality with men, that, according to Gustav, was egoism.

The third arena in which women's efforts were focused represented "more amorphous and broad-ranging activities toward women's self-determination via 'emancipation' from structures, conventions, and attitudes enforced by law and custom."[32] Here, again, Gustav probably felt the changing American culture in general and the attitudes of women in particular to be a threat to all he had been taught, all he believed about women's roles in society.

The conflict between Gustav's rigid German thinking and his practice is evident from his pronouncements on women's emancipation and his advocacy of the deaconess movement in his denomination. For Gustav Niebuhr, emancipation was equated with women's "enjoyment, respect, freedom, and sport, together with freedom from all the burdensome duties and responsibilities."[33]

The growth of feminism as a movement of consciousness is seen in the beginning of the twentieth century. It was not the result of carefree activities absolved from duty and responsibility. "Feminism intended to transform the ideas of submission and femininity that had been inculcated in women."[34] A community to support this struggle was found in the suffrage movement. Gradual changes in thinking can be documented.

> Nineteenth-century spokeswomen had voiced women's individuality of temperament, unpredetermined by gender or by family role, as at least a minor and sometimes a major theme. Individualism—in the sense of self-development—became much more pronounced in the Feminism of the 1910s....By the early twentieth century it was a commonplace that the New Woman stood for self-development as contrasted to self-sacrifice or submergence in the family.[35]

Descriptions of Hulda such as "mirror image" and "in the footsteps of her mother" by Niebuhr biographers reveal the image of a dutiful daughter, a good German girl, just as Gustav had envisioned. Hulda's own statement that a college education was not assumed for girls enabled her to live with her father's lack of educational expectations for her. Hulda made her point most clearly when in her letter to June Bingham she said, " I was very fully occupied." It sounds like a footnote, almost as if she were saying, "don't think I wasn't busy, that I didn't have my work." Hulda was careful not to leave the impression that her own self-development was sacrificed due to her submergence in the family.

Women's self-sacrifice was looked upon very differently by Gustav when he wrote in 1908:

> This praiseworthy striving of the modern woman for higher education is confronted by the sad fact that cultured, well-educated men, according to English statistics—particularly the most learned men—generally have an inexplicable, deeply-rooted tendency to avoid learned women and to choose instead of a college-trained competent young lady an inexperienced, uneducated, fun-oriented young girl, causing us to fear that even the attempt to secure higher education for all young women could in the end serve only to increase enormously the demand for such fresh young girls.[36]

Gustav's contrast of the emancipated English or American woman, the learned, college-educated woman, with the more modest, fun-oriented German woman is useful in understanding the separate sphere he envisioned for women in the home and in the church.

The women's movement found in the Protestant faith "another important generator and legitimator of women's social assertions."[37] Though many Protestant denominations were involved in the establishment of women's colleges in the late nineteenth century, it was proselytizing, evangelical Protestants who "elevated and endorsed women's moral character and social role."[38]

The German Evangelical Synod demonstrates how one immigrant denomination sought to establish its faith tradition in the United States and the special role it sought for women. Gustav Niebuhr entered the denominational seminary of the German Evangelical synod of North America in 1883 when there were 535 churches and 427 pastors.[39] The denomination, representing a union in the United States of separate Lutheran and Reformed religious traditions in Germany, sought to spread its evangelical faith in ministry with German immigrants. The denomination was concerned with three main objectives: establishing new churches, encouraging education, and initiating social ministry.

In his analysis of the role of immigrant churches in the United States, John Bodnar notes that

> it is difficult to cling to notions of the church as extension of tradition which simply retarded adaptation to a modern, capitalistic, secular society or even as an agent which simply fostered modernization and Americanization. At the very least it was both of these.[40]

While this is true of the Evangelical denomination, its theological commitment to leadership in social transformation in the culture made the church more an agent of change, fostering immigrants' transition to their new land.

The church's emphasis on new congregations, education, and social witness are specific examples of how the denomination served as an agent of assimilation for German immigrants. From the beginning of its organization, the denomination emphasized and required an educated clergy. Both Reinhold and H. Richard spent their high school years in the synod's proseminary, Elmhurst College, preparing to attend Eden Theological Seminary near St. Louis.

Equally important was the education of children. "There was hardly a congregation so small or so poor that it did not have either a schoolhouse or a schoolroom attached to church or parsonage."[41] Adolph Baltzer, president of the synod, visited among the churches in 1868. His report contained comments about the religious education of children, providing a portrait of one of the major priorities of the denomination.

> There is no question that over a large area of our Synod there is to be found an eager desire for the establishment and maintenance of parochial schools, so essential to the life and progress of our congregations.... We frequently hear complaints about what is happening to our young people after confirmation—how frivolous they are, often defiant of restraint, paying little heed to religion.... We should leave untried no method that has been found helpful in dealing with the problem—such as organizing a young men's society under competent leadership, providing good reading matter, and bringing the witness of God's Word to bear on the idea of Christian family life, especially in Sunday school and in regular services of worship for the youth of the church.[42]

The church's commitment to religious education is obvious in the statistics that illustrate the denomination's growth in numbers of pastors, churches, parochial schools, and Sunday schools. Between the years 1854 and 1883 the number of churches grew from 149 to 557. Of these congregations, 20 had parochial schools in 1854 and 266 churches had schools in 1883. The number of churches that had Sunday schools grew from 17 in 1854 to 412 in 1883. Sunday school attendance grew from 1,141 in 1854 to 41, 588 in 1883.[43]

Another indicator of the importance of religious education was the production of resource materials for use in parochial schools and Sunday schools. A German primer and reader were first available in 1868. In 1874, the General Conference approved for publication a book of Bible stories, *Biblische Geschicten,* and a hymnbook was published in 1882. Given this context, Hulda's leadership in the Sunday school and her role as a teacher in the parochial school were valued activities that contributed both to the development of religious faith and Christian character. As she said herself, "I was fully occupied." Inherent in that statement is the belief in her own self-development and the contribution she was making to the lives of young people in the church.

A third focus of the denomination was on ministry to sick and disabled persons. Gustav was a leader in the establishment of the Emmaus Asylum, an institution for the treatment and care of persons with epilepsy. Such efforts in "home mission," as it was referred to by the denomination, were modelled upon similar institutions in Germany.[44] The deaconess movement was initiated in Germany in 1836 to train women to work in hospitals and homes.

THE VOCATION OF DEACONESS

In 1902, when the Niebuhr family moved to Lincoln, Illinois, where Gustav was called to serve as pastor for St. John's Church, he also managed the newly built deaconess home and hospital. A priority for Gustav's work was the recruiting and training of deaconesses who were to serve as "servants of the Lord Jesus, servants of the sick and poor for Jesus' sake, and servants to each other."[45] Theodore Fliedner, a pastor in Germany, developed the thesis supporting this model of ministry that "women have a special gift for service."[46] Such a vocational opportunity was progressive in its day in Germany, offering women an opportunity to work outside the home in an era when such possibilities were scarce.

Beginning with a focus on nursing, the deaconess movement soon developed into a broader understanding of ministry. Christian Golder helped to create the role of deaconess in the German Methodist church and was a coworker with Gustav. She identified four areas of work for the deaconess: teaching, nursing, parish deaconess, and missionary deaconess.[47]

In 1902, the *Lincoln Courier* included an article that clearly states Gustav's agenda.

While the Deaconess home in Lincoln will be called a hospital and house for afflicted people, yet the future may see it expand into a training school, where candidates may broaden their education and training in various lines and become teachers. The field is a wide territory and the movement is new but those in charge believe their ambition will be realized. Young ladies...will come forward to assist this worthy cause, fostered by the Church, to preach the ethics of a true religion.[48]

Gustav did not believe women should seek an education because such self-development was egoistic. Deaconess training involved service to others, making it an acceptable vocation for young women. As religious training, according to Gustav, it would foster the kind of development in women that would sustain the family and the church in a day when both institutions were facing great changes.

Gustav's passionate zeal for the deaconess movement served as an outlet for his beliefs about women and the family and their role in society, views that he found increasingly threatened by the women's movement.

> The movement for women's liberation with its aversion to family duties, to the blessing of children, and above all to humble service will, I fear, eventually become the greatest curse of this nation, otherwise so richly blessed.[49]

He not only equated women's education and self-development with egoism but eventually came to the conclusion that such self-development would result in the death of Christian faith in women.[50]

In 1904 in *Evangelischer Diakonissonfreund*, a publication of the Evangelical Synod, Gustav expanded his understanding of the purpose of the deaconess movement.

> In this servant form everything is contained that finally determines the character also of the diaconate of women.... The apostle Paul already proposes the idea that it were better for the young woman not to marry since she would be less handicapped in serving the Lord...for the service of the Lord is a blessedness, and whoever serves the Lord most is most blessed. Since a wife can serve the Lord only in a thoroughly Christian family, and since such families to this day are the exception, it follows that the advice of the apostle still is completely justified.[51]

It was difficult for Gustav to recruit young women to serve as deaconesses at a time when the culture was slowly beginning to offer new opportunities for women in education and in other vocations in the world of work outside the home. He made public his theology—that the new roles for women in American life were unbiblical and would lead to the destruction of the home and religious faith—in order to keep women of his church committed to their religious calling.[52]

There is no evidence, however, that Gustav encouraged or expected his daughter to enter deaconess training. That may have been more an issue for her mother, Lydia, and Hulda's aunt, Adele Hosto, who was ordained a deaconess. Two observations about Hulda's life at this critical time in her development provide useful insights about familial influence. In some unfinished "conversations" Ursula Niebuhr reflects on her life with Reinhold:

> Hulda, your older sister, again was very much influenced by your father. German Protestant churches as the more evangelical wing of the Church of England had been influenced by the movement which reestablished deaconesses to serve and to minister the church.... Your aunt, your mother's younger sister, Adele, after she had done her

nursing training was ordained a deaconess. Hulda, your sister, apparently went through an agonizing time as an older adolescent wondering if she ought to follow the same vocation. I wonder who it was who released her from that felt imperative? Did your mother have the wisdom and common sense, and know it was not for her?[53]

Family correspondence gives no indication that Hulda felt this imperative. Chrystal commented about the relationship between father and daughter:

Gustav...insensitively forced his talented daughter Hulda to endure the hell born of not understanding and supporting her desire for higher education. That she eventually succeeded in obtaining one is a tribute to her ability and resolve. Yet insensitive though he was, it is apparent that Hulda's maturation coincided with a movement that Gustav believed endangered the Christian faith itself.[54]

Given that the predominating attitude was that a college education would make a woman even more fit as a homemaker, Hulda's father believed precisely the opposite. Though he did not discourage her from going to college, she did not receive the same support or emotional encouragement as did her brothers. Though never responding publicly to her father's belief about women and their role in society, Hulda quietly, diligently, and with great commitment followed her dream of an education and a vocation.

Whatever else was communicated to Hulda from her father, she knew inside that she was bright, talented, and possessed gifts as a scholar, musician, and teacher. A transcript of her credits from Lincoln High School shows she had four credits in English, one in history, two in Latin, two in German, one in bookkeeping, two in music, two and one-half in science (physiology, chemistry, and physics), and one and one-half in math (algebra and geometry).

Hulda's silence at this early stage of development could only be identified with obeying her father's wishes for her career, which was to be patterned after her mother's. She listened to that voice, that external authority, for six years after graduating from high school. Then, in 1912, she took her future into her own hands and entered college.

Hulda began her higher education at Lincoln College in their family hometown of Lincoln, Illinois, in 1912, one year before Gustav's death. She was twenty-three at the time and living at home with her parents. Besides her many responsibilities at St. John's, her father's church, she also was hired to teach for two years in the church's parochial school. Much later Hulda commented on the beginnings of her college education.

I took courses in Lincoln College but was too involved in the needs of home and church after high school graduation to do full time work. After my father's death I worked a number of years to earn my way through a course in Boston (or whatever school it would be where I could specialize in religious education). Most of the time, in Lincoln and chiefly in Detroit, that work was in newspaper offices. Always I was active in the church school, usually heading up the elementary work. For some time I directed the county work of Logan County.[55]

While Hulda began college work, the family was supporting the education of Reinhold at Eden Seminary and H. Richard's proseminary studies at Elmhurst College. Walter had attended college briefly at Illinois Wesleyan but left after one year.

Gustav's death in April 1913 no doubt played some part in the interruption of her education since she and her mother were left without any financial support. Because it was no longer possible for Hulda and Lydia to live in the church manse, the money from Gustav's insurance was used to build a house for Lydia and Hulda in Lincoln. Ursula Niebuhr remembers this time in Hulda's life as one where she was suddenly without a job or vocation.

She had not been trained to earn, and I remember you told me how conscientious she was going to night school and learning to type, so that she could get some poor-paying job, addressing envelopes and licking stamps until she could save enought to take more academic training.[56]

To understand the process that enabled the development of her self-identity and freedom of vocational choice, the relationship between mother and daughter must be closely examined.

"WARM LITTLE FRICTIONS"

Hulda's individuation within and from the Niebuhr family involved the tasks of both self-development and self-identity. Her self-development was achieved as she struggled with the conflict between her own educational and career goals and those envisioned by her father. Her self-identity was a critical issue in her relationship with her mother. Other than the eleven years, 1918-1929, when she was in Boston, Hulda and her mother never lived apart until Hulda's death in 1959. After Gustav's death, Lydia was dependent on her children for financial and emotional support as well as for a place to live.

Ursula Niebuhr has raised the question about Hulda's freedom in choosing her own identity considering her father's expectations and her

close association with her mother. Christopher Niebuhr, son of Ursula and
Reinhold Niebuhr, has added another dimension to the issue of influence on
Hulda. "She [Hulda] rejected deaconess training suggested by my
grandmother's sister [Adele Hosto]. The school was Hulda's contribution,
my grandmother's goal was deaconess work."[57]

Christopher Niebuhr has suggested that Lydia might have envisioned
Hulda following in her footsteps, receiving church training and becoming
officially what had been Lydia's unofficial function all her life: a parish
worker, assistant to a pastor. Hulda chose to complete her education rather
than entering deaconess training.

The picture that emerges of Hulda Niebuhr at age twenty-three is that of
a young, intelligent woman who, like many others in her day, was struggling
with the question of whom she was as an individual and what she was going
to do with her life.

The family "cloud of witnesses" that surrounded Hulda represented a
variety of models for her future. On one side was the role model of her
mother, tireless parish assistant to her husband, an example of what the
deaconess assistant became in the local church. On another side was her
aunt, Adele Hosto, only eight years older than Hulda, who began deaconess
training while Gustav was still alive and who was ordained shortly after his
death. Her father's expectations, in some ways more negative than positive,
were clearly in evidence. The young man that Gustav had envisioned would
marry his daughter had not appeared. Hulda had neither found her career, as
her brother Walter had with newspaper reporting and publishing, nor had
one intentionally been selected for her, as was true of her brothers Reinhold
and H. Richard.

Ursula Niebuhr's question mentioned earlier in this chapter is important
to reconsider. With all these influences, who released Hulda from "felt
imperatives"? Was it her mother? Lydia, as much as Gustav, provided
important and influential "starting points" for the children. Gustav's
contribution to their intellectual development lay in his language instruction
and his scholarship. His energy, forcefulness, and pietistic faith contributed
to the nature and direction of the Niebuhrs' formation as a family. Lydia's
contribution to their intellectual development lay in her musical and artistic
abilities. Her energy and enthusiasm were conveyed through her commitment to the growth of her children as human beings, an important aspect in
their formation in and individuation from their family.

In the Niebuhr family, one style of parenting was not more important than
another. Together, the blending of Lydia and Gustav's complementary
styles nurtured both the abstract and cognitive as well as the artistic and
intuitive abilities in their children. In a introduction to an article written by

Gustav Niebuhr, Chrystal said that he "stands as a reminder to us that scholars are not only people of genius, but are those who are raised in homes where that genius is cultivated."[58]

The Niebuhr home was one where the children's intelligence, creativity, and religious faith were encouraged to develop. The Niebuhr home was not a place of silence. Creative activity, drama, music, language studies and dialog were at the heart of family activities. The children were encouraged to communicate, to test their abilities, to serve as leaders, and to find their voice.

In a day that faced change in the family, in women's lives and in the influence the church had on the culture, the Niebuhrs intentionally nurtured their children to follow the Christian faith tradition that they believed would make a difference in the world. For Gustav and Lydia, it mattered what their children believed and how that belief was practiced in daily life.

In reflecting on the earlier list of values of the Niebuhr family, Lydia's role in each of those is as strong or stronger than Gustav's. She probably had more influence on the growth and development of her children than Gustav did between 1892 and 1902 when he was busy working with the church and home in Wright City, Missouri. Lydia equalled Gustav's energy and commitment in her job within the family and the church. In describing their first congregation in San Francisco, St. John's, Fox noted that

> before the marriage Gustav had sometimes preached to congregations of two or three. With Lydia's full-time aid—and musical talent—his parish began to grow. Lydia, one of twelve children, knew all about church operations. She had already served her father as organist and Sunday School assistant.[59]

From her father's perspective, Hulda's call in life was relational—to help her mother and to work in the church until that time when she would care for her husband and her children. The latter never happened.

Nancy Chodorow cites a book by Signe Hammer, *Daughters and Mothers: Mothers and Daughters*, that describes "how issues of primary identification, oneness and separateness follow mother-daughter pairs from a daughter's earliest infancy until she is well into being a mother or even grandmother herself."[60]

Fox suggested that Hulda was a "mirror image" of her mother. In similar fashion Chrystal suggested that Hulda followed completely in her mother's footsteps. These statements are not convincing. Rather, Hulda's individuation and differentiation took place after the death of her father when she put herself through college and graduate school. Though closely identified with her mother, Hulda made new footsteps from the legacies inherited from both her mother and father.

In 1929, Hulda wrote a book of "verse and doggerel," as she called it, as a Christmas gift for her mother. A poem in it reveals some of her thoughts about her family.

Warm Little Frictions

This strange city is so cold,—
Everyone speaks so smoothly to me.
What a comfort they were,
The "warm little frictions of home!"

At home
Someone would have told me
That I had let my shoulders
Become stooped,
That my opinions on the state of the universe
Need some amendments;
And I must practice more, for my last solo
Was not my best;
That my new hat, so proudly worn
Was not too wisely chosen.

But here.
No one loves me enough
To take the twinkle to disagree
With me;
No one cares sufficiently
To take the chance
Of hurting me:
"How perfectly lovely!"
"How absolutely correct!"

I did not know what a comfort they were,
The "warm little frictions of home"

And how chilly it would be
Away from the love that is their source.[61]

For Hulda the family was a source of love and support. It was also a place of honesty and reality as suggested by her phrase, "the warm little frictions of home." The Niebuhr home was obviously a place where, as Richard R. Niebuhr has suggested, the family members, while sometimes disagreeing, strengthened and shaped one another and thus enabled their individuation.

Hulda and Lydia, c. 1904

2

Claiming a Career (1918–1928)

THE YEAR 1918 PROVED TO BE an important one of transition in Hulda's life. She took a significant step in focusing on her growth and professional development. Grounded with years of experiential education in the church, Hulda made the decision to leave her work at Bethel Church and to continue her formal education. She seemed concerned at this point in her life with claiming a vocational path.

Most likely there were several voices seeking to influence her. Hulda's aunt, Adele Hosto, would have encouraged her to enter deaconess training, for she believed that "it is evident that in no other branch of the work can a deaconess serve God in such manifold ways as are opened to her within the confines of a large city parish which offers an abundance and variety of work."[1] Lydia believed that work in the church as a religious educator with responsibilities for teaching and administration of Sunday and weekday programs was a fulfilling and challenging career. Hulda's brothers might have encouraged her to continue her education. Hulda's library contained a copy of *A Social Theory of Religious Education,* by George Albert Coe, that has the inscription, "To Sis from H R Niebuhr, Christmas 1922."

Hulda does not appear as selfless at this point in her life; she appears as a woman whose self-development had taken a self-imposed moratorium to help ease her family through a difficult transition. But in the midst of the surrounding voices, Hulda made a decision to claim her context and place and for the first time to choose a life for herself. The journey to Boston and the School of Religious Education and Social Service of Boston University helped Hulda begin to name her theory of religious education and to establish her identity apart from her mother and her brothers.

A FAMILY IN TRANSITION

The future for the Niebuhrs as a family became apparent soon after Gustav's death in 1913. H. Richard was in St. Louis studying at Eden Seminary. Walter was an investor and editor at the *Courier*, a newspaper in Lincoln, Illinois. His debts with the paper had finally overwhelmed him and Reinhold was left to pick up the financial burden of the family, including providing housing for his mother and sister. On August 8, 1915, Reinhold moved to Detroit where he became the pastor of Bethel Evangelical Church. Founded in August 1912, by 1915 its membership included 65 and the congregation had purchased a small chapel. It was considered a "mission church" for new, young pastors. During Reinhold's pastorate at Bethel from 1915 to 1928, the membership grew from 65 to 656. The Sunday school enrollment started at 52 and reached 428 by 1928.

Lydia joined Reinhold in Detroit in January 1916 and "immediately took over much of the day-to-day conduct of the parish, including the Sunday school and the choir."[2] As Fox has noted, such activities on Lydia's part freed Reinhold to write articles and to pursue speaking engagements that helped to supplement the meager salary that Bethel was able to pay him. "More important than money was influence for his ideas and notice for his person. He could feel at home in a church only if one foot was firmly planted outside of it."[3] The opposite was true for Lydia. She felt at home and her equilibrium was in balance only when both of her feet were planted firmly inside the church.

The church recognized Lydia's distinctive contribution to its religious education program. The congregation seemed to understand Lydia as having a call to their church. "In January, 1916, Mrs. Lydia Niebuhr, the pastor's mother, came to assist her son in his work in the church. The fine work which she did for so many years is well-known to all. She helped to lay a strong foundation which has lasted to this day."[4]

Hulda moved to Detroit in 1917 to help her mother with the educational work at Bethel Church. The twenty-fifth anniversary booklet of Bethel Evangelical Church provides evidence of the scope of Lydia's and Hulda's responsibilities in the church.

Teachers were induced to join training classes due largely to the efforts of the pastor's mother, Mrs. Lydia Niebuhr; and able help was given by his sister, Miss Hulda Niebuhr. The fact that the Bible School membership during the years 1916 to 1920 exceeded that of the church reflected the efforts of the Niebuhr family and the corps of workers whose loyalty they succeeded so well in winning.[5]

In a description of the Bethel Sunday School, thanks is given to Lydia Niebuhr, who "gave of her time and effort and accepted the challenge for the leadership of this school."[6] The church took pride in describing its Sunday school as one committed to "progressive religious education," meaning a commitment to effective administration and training for teachers in the Sunday school. Its teachers were enrolled in training schools in Detroit and were "recognized leaders in the field of religion in this city and the State of Michigan."[7] The administration of the Sunday school included supervision of all ages organized into departments, preschool through adult. Another important part of the missionary education of the Sunday school was daily vacation Bible school offered for children during the summer months.

As the religious education program grew, help was needed in administration. Hulda supplied that need. Hulda's position was probably that of assistant to the "assistant pastor," her mother. Besides aiding her mother in responsibilities with the Sunday school, daily vacation Bible school, and the junior choir, Hulda helped with the children's sermon during the worship service. "Often Niebuhr [Reinhold] turned the children's sermon over to his sister, Hulda, whose gifts lay noticeably in that direction."[8] When she left the church in 1918, Hulda's departure created a large gap at a time when the Sunday school enrollment was larger than the church membership.

For Lydia herself, the pastoral duties of welcoming visitors and visiting those who were sick and shut-in were also included in her unofficial job description. Florence Schulz, a member of Bethel Evangelical Church, recalled her welcome to Detroit and the congregation.

The whole congregation and the minister and his mother welcomed us with open arms.... Being new in town Mother Niebuhr took me under her wing. Such love and kindness was most welcome.[9]

AN INHERITED THEORY OF RELIGIOUS EDUCATION

Lydia passed on to her daughter both a theory of religious education and a model for one who assisted the pastor. In an article she wrote for a National Convocation of Evangelical Sunday Schools in 1919, Lydia made clear her theory of religious education when she identified four purposes of Sunday school work. The first was teaching.

> The greatest danger of religious education is the danger of teaching vague ideals, general truths, in words and by examples which are so broad and loose that they have no real meaning for the pupil.... Activities which teach service, love, helpfulness, cooperation are a very necessary part of Christian Education.[10]

A second purpose of the Sunday school was to foster a social spirit. By this she meant the building of Christian community. Such community, she believed, didn't just happen but was the result of common work that brought people together.

> Our children and our grown-ups will learn much more about cooperation by working together than they will in a month of Sunday school instruction. In the short hour of a Sunday morning session there is no chance for real fellowship, for mutual appreciation, for forgetting grudges and for forming friendship. But this is a major part of religious education that men should become as members of the same family.[11]

Lydia also believed this spirit of community had important implications for the relationship between teacher and pupil.

> We can never be successful teachers unless we love those whom we teach, have a genuine understanding of their characters, their capabilities, their difficulties and their fine qualities. We do not learn to know them in visits or in Sunday morning hours, but when we work with them and allow them to be their natural, unfettered selves.[12]

A third purpose was to teach members to behave in a Christian manner. "There is absolutely no value in our teaching if it does not issue in life and character."[13] Lydia, as a longtime teacher of young people, realized that Christian behavior was learned through experience. It didn't come through lectures or lessons but through participation in a church group. She believed each person in the Sunday school was important. When a child is interested, "it makes him a part of the whole, giving him a share in the ownership of the concern."[14] She valued the learners' contributions to the learning process. The ideas and creativity that the learners brought were as important as those of the teacher.

A fourth purpose of religious education was to provide weekday activities for children and young people. Such additional programs would connect visitors with the school and the church. Lydia believed the activities also had the advantage of allowing children freer expression.

> It seems to me that the boys and girls are quite a bit more their natural selves after they have come from school and work than on a Sunday morning when they have been aroused with the special purpose of getting to Sunday school in time and have been incased in their finest and most uncomfortable clothes. There is a freer atmosphere, a more natural attitude of give and take between them.[15]

While Lydia embodied the vision that she articulated in her theory of religious education, the legacy she left to Hulda was more than just the role of a professional religious educator, which was an acceptable vocation for a woman in that day. Because of her relationships with her father, husband, and son, Lydia's role had been expanded to include responsibilities in areas that today would be labeled as evangelism and pastoral care. Ralph Abele, an assistant pastor who had worked with Reinhold and Lydia, shared this observation regarding Lydia, which was revealing in its assumptions about women's spheres:

> If there is anything more than another that the people of congregation long for from the woman of the parsonage, it is firm and quiet strength devoid of ostentation, assurance of understanding, a capacity to see and to help do what most needs doing, be it ever so simple, ever so hard. Mrs. Niebuhr gave the people of Bethel that.[16]

Lydia was an extrovert, a woman possessing an incredible amount of energy, enthusiasm, creativity, and zest for life. She went about her tasks with great commitment. She did not seem to need accolades or recognition for her work. Lydia delighted in being with people and enabling them to feel part of a group, a family, a church community. Essential to her emotional health was purpose in life. She gained her meaning through the lives and careers of her family members. Lydia grew up in an era and was associated with a vocation that provided limited options for the gifts and talents that women had to offer. She, probably more than many women her age, was able to achieve a certain amount of independence and fulfillment in her career as unofficial "assistant pastor."

What then did she pass on to her daughter both personally and professionally? Many of those who knew both women have suggested the importance of understanding the nature of their relationship.

Hulda, at a critical time in her life as an adolescent, was not encouraged by her parents to establish an identity separate from her mother but was encouraged by her father to become like her mother. While confirming Hulda's dependence on her family for vocational direction and identity, her parents, by the kind of education and nurturing environment they provided, encouraged her intellectual and creative development and individuation. Perhaps it was this knowledge of her gifts and abilities that enabled Hulda to survive the physical closeness to her mother while achieving at the same time her own identity as a professional woman. Ursula Niebuhr, Hulda's sister-in-law, has observed that

> she was bound with the shackles of the vicarage or parsonage, and yet at times, I think, would have liked to have flown away, far away from it, and enjoyed life outside the parish and the parsonage. The mother, Lydia Niebuhr, was married in her 16th year and had all her children before she was 21. Hulda being the eldest was therefore less than 20 years younger than her mother. Perhaps this made them too closely associated in their interests and in the views of others. Mrs. Niebuhr was...gifted with small children, which, no doubt, restrained Hulda from branching out into a wider world of experience.[17]

Was Hulda's close relationship with her mother restrictive or empowering? Ursula Niebuhr suggests that their close association might have prevented Hulda from pursuing other vocational options. But Hulda shared with her mother a joy and excitement in working with children and contributing to their intellectual and faith development. Perhaps Lydia's model offered to Hulda a profession that would accept and challenge her natural gifts and abilities as an educator.

Other than the ten years when she lived in Boston, 1918 to 1928, Lydia and Hulda were never physically apart for long periods of time. So the questions remain: Who influenced whom? Who was the more independent in the relationship? What did Lydia represent for Hulda? Were their selves continuous? Was Hulda's separation and differentiation from her mother expected, encouraged, supported, discouraged?

Hulda left a clue about their relationship in a poem she wrote while in Boston, a birthday greeting for her mother in 1922.

The Spirit of Home

Boston has some mammoth buildings,
Many ships that go to sea—
Just as the place I come from,
But they don't spell home to me.

There are hosts of dashing autos
And of Fords the streets to roam—
As in the place I come from
Still, they don't make Boston home.

But there is a little lady
Living where I must not be—
Living in the place I come from
And her name spells home to me.

She can love you though she knows you,
Though she sees much froth and foam,
Hold you to the best that's in you—
She's the spirit of the home.

I am glad that lady's spirit
Is not tied to any place—
It can help to make at-home-ness
Though I cannot see her face.

I don't need the ships and autos
Mammoth buildings spire and dome,—
Let me have the little lady

Who's the spirit of the home.[18]

For Hulda, her mother represented a self-taught, wise, and loving parent, the "spirit of the home," who accepted her for whom she was, while also expecting her to live up to her potential. "Spirit" is an accurate way to describe what Lydia meant to her daughter.

Lydia provided a sense of balance and day-to-day maintenance of the household that enabled Hulda, who was physically fragile (allergies and a bad back) and who had a more introverted personality, to make her way in the world as a single professional woman. Lydia served to reproduce Hulda, to care for her, providing social outlets and enabling community.[19] It was *Mütterchen*, as Lydia was called by the family, who did the cooking, sewed

Hulda's clothes, and kept up with the daily events of the house and the world.

At this point in their lives together, their selves were more continuous than distinct. Hulda was following in her mother's footsteps, aiding and supporting Lydia and her brother Reinhold in their work at Bethel Church.

AN EDUCATIONAL QUEST

Hulda Niebuhr took a bold step in search of answers to her vocational quest in 1918. For the next ten years she studied and taught in the School of Religious Education and Social Service at Boston University. Besides earning two degrees, Hulda taught courses and was the principal of the weekday school.

Hulda was not unlike other women of her day who were struggling to identify their own vocational future. In 1918, when she entered Boston University as an undergraduate, Hulda was twenty-nine, probably ten years older than some of her classmates. She was also a single woman at an age when many women were already married with children. For these women, education had served to prepare them for their work as homemakers.

Hulda Niebuhr's life and vocation evidenced both similarities to and differences from the struggles of other women in the 1920s. For the most part middle- and upper-class women were more educated and believed that family life should not interfere with their careers. In the twenties, over 80 percent of college students graduating from women's colleges were getting married. Thirty years earlier the figure was 50 percent.[20] Women's roles in society changed dramatically as they began to see the possibility for new options for their lives. Carl Degler has observed that at the beginning of the twentieth century, women had a choice to make between marriage or a career, "since it was unlikely they could have both."[21] For many women in the 1920s, especially those in the upper classes, marriage and employment represented a less threatening position to take in confronting "gender injustices" within traditional settings of the family and the workplace.

The issue seemed to be focused not on equality of education as much as on equality of opportunity in the workplace and on the traditional understandings of marriage supported by both laws and custom. In 1890, 35 percent of college students were women. By the 1920s, women represented almost half the college population. Whereas in the 1890s women who went to college tended to remain single or to marry later in life, in the twentieth century college-educated women were marrying in greater numbers and at younger ages.[22]

Women in the 1920s encountered a culture embedded in unjust gender practices. For example, a study by the National Education Association reported that 60 percent of school boards in 1,532 cities polled had discriminatory policies toward married women. A single woman teacher who decided to get married was forced to resign. "Since teaching was the principal occupation of college-educated women at the time, such policy amounted to a class-based proscription against gainful employment for middle-class wives."[23]

Women faced an unfavorable welcome in the labor market where their devaluation was obvious in the lack of equal pay. In the midst of struggling with voices speaking to them about responsibility to their family, women found little support for their attempts to combine a career outside the home with their family life and its requirements inside the home.

In focusing on a career in education, Hulda had chosen a profession amenable to the employment of women. "The number of women college teachers multiplied six times between 1910 and 1930."[24] Further, through her particular focus on religious education, she had chosen a vocational path close to the heart of her mother.

Hulda, who paid for all her education, was probably unlike other women attending college then in terms of financial support. Education for middle- and upper-class women in the twenties had finally become more of the norm and less the exception. Mothers who had either been denied or fought to have an education were interested in providing one for their daughters. When the fear that women's education would destroy the family had finally subsided, higher education for women became more acceptable. Charles McIver, an educator in North Carolina, noted close to the end of the nineteenth century what society wanted to hear and believe: If you "educate a man, you educated one person; educate a mother and you have educated the whole family."[25]

Hulda's decision to complete her interrupted college education involved several decisions. She was literally leaving home for the first time in her life, moving away from the dominating influence of her mother and the legacy of her father's autocratic beliefs about women's role in society.

She was leaving her work in Detroit at Bethel Evangelical Church as Reinhold's assistant. She might have been seeking to lighten the burden on her family, since Reinhold had become financially responsible not only for his mother and sister but also for his brother Walter.[26] Hulda's decision to leave Detroit and move to Boston offered her the chance to find her voice as she journeyed outside the family to claim a career.

THE KIND OF WOMANHOOD SHE REPRESENTS

Besides her family, the other institution that contributed to Hulda Niebuhr's formation and to her vocational identity were the schools in which she studied and taught. Boston University is the first of those institutions that contributed to her process of individuation. Religious education at Boston University when Hulda Niebuhr was a student grew out of the vision of Walter Scott Athearn who went to Boston University in 1916 at age forty-four, taking with him a wealth of experience in education.

Athearn had entered the profession as a teacher and served as a principal of public schools in Iowa, as associate professor of pedagogy at Drake University and as dean of the Highland Park Normal College. He was the founder and first dean of the School of Religious Education of Boston University. He was described as one who had been "a pioneer in the religious education field and established the first department of religious education for college credit in the United States."[27]

Athearn and Boston University came together at an optimum moment in history. Athearn had a dream for the professionalization of the religious educator. He was seeking to create an educational program grounded in a balance of theory and practice. Courses to be offered would have direct relationship to vocational or career paths. Such an educational program would exhibit the kind of organization and administration it was teaching. Administrators and professors would be expected to share their knowledge and expertise through publishing their writings. Athearn was seeking to turn an extension program into a standardized academic school.

A poem she wrote during her years in Boston, "So Much To Do," accurately describes Hulda Niebuhr's life during these formative years. In this poem Hulda describes the activities and demands of each day of the week. Such activities included teacher's meetings, visits with friends, and church responsibilities. Her description of Sunday illustrates the tempo of her life at this time.

Sunday

Yes, Pastor. I will try and see
That Wednesday I can present be.
I really did not mean to shirk
But I was quite weighed down with work.
At home, as in the office too
There always is so much to do.[28]

In 1918 Hulda enrolled in the Boston University School of Religious Education and Social Service to pursue a bachelor of religious education degree. For the first time in her life she had an opportunity to exert her leadership. She was able to emerge from the shadow of her mother and her brothers and begin to claim the power of her own voice. She completed thirty-five courses in three years, graduating in 1922. The courses she took represented a balance of the fields of study with a special focus on teaching methods and working with kindergarten- and elementary-age children.

While still a student, Hulda became a critic teacher in the Boston University demonstration weekday school in 1921. The Boston University Year Book for 1922 to 1925 described this course as one that "deals with analysis and constructive criticism of classroom teaching, building of curriculum, observation and analysis of pupil growth."[29] It was offered for students in the degree program and also for teachers in the demonstration school.

Immediately after graduation, Hulda enrolled in the graduate program of Boston University, pursuing a master of arts degree in the university rather than in the School of Religious Education and Social Service. One possible reason for this is that by 1921, before receiving her degree, she had already been hired to teach in the demonstration school.

By 1922, she was listed as an instructor in the elementary education part of the division of religious education in the School of Religious Education and Social Service. She was also serving as director of the demonstration school. She may have been advised by Walter Athearn, with whom she worked on an independent study during the summer of 1921, that it would be best not to pursue graduate study in the school in which she was teaching. She also may have been seeking a broader curriculum for her studies than she could have found in the specialized curriculum there.

Hulda's course work in the School of Education and the School of Religious Education was focused on teaching methods, child development, and administration and supervision of teaching.

She spent the summers of 1923 and 1925 studying in the summer school of the University of Chicago, taking three courses each summer. Her courses were Supervision of Kindergarten-Primary Children, Psychology of Learning, Methods of Teaching Ideals, and the Psychological Basis of Ethics.[30] She also took Systematic Theology and Modern Christian Social Movement in the Divinity School.

Hulda gives insight into why she pursued the master of arts degree in her "Professional and Academic Record" prepared for McCormick Theological Seminary. "During these later years [1922-28] [I] studied every summer in the University of Chicago in psychology, education, philosophy, choosing courses I needed for my work rather than only such as grouped under a Master's degree in religious education."[31] She also explained why she completed five of the six courses taken at the University of Chicago. "Boston did not accept more than 5 points from Chicago, but I had more points in Boston than in Chicago."[32] No reason is given by Hulda as to why she spent two summers in school at the University of Chicago, transferring this credit to her graduate program at Boston University. One possible reason could have been the desire to broaden her study, since Chicago at this time was considered to be one of the centers for religious education along with Boston and New York.

After receiving her bachelor's degree in religious education, Hulda began to teach more courses in the Children's Division Specialization in the Religious Education Section of the curriculum in the School of Religious Education and Social Service. In addition to the course for critic teachers, she taught Observation and Practice Teaching, which included one hour of classroom instruction, observation of children's activities, and practice teaching in the demonstration school.[33] By 1925, Hulda was listed as assistant professor in the *Boston University Bulletin* that described course offerings for the school year 1925–26.

The School of Religious Education and Social Service maintained laboratories for observation and practice work. Its administrators believed that "all theory courses should be accompanied by practical laboratory courses, and that all practice work, to be of value, should be under careful supervision."[34] Laboratory experiences were provided for those persons studying church administration and institutional work such as settlement houses, industrial schools, and missions. Laboratories were also provided for home missionary situations—medical mission, deaconess homes, courts, hospitals, prisons, and reformatories were also used to provide experiences for students.

In addition, the School of Religious Education and Social Service had two training schools: laboratory schools "where conditions are largely controlled for purposes of scientific experimentation" and apprenticeship schools "in which pupils who have had practice in demonstration schools under expert guidance may have practice under normal conditions."[35]

At the same time that she was teaching and finishing her degree work, taking four courses in 1925–26 and one course in 1926–27, Hulda also worked on her thesis, "Children's Lies: A Psychological Study with Special Reference to German Source Material," completing it during the first term of 1927–28. It explored the role that lying plays in helping children know what is true and what is false, how to express that understanding, and the role of the environment in the growth process.[36]

Also during 1927–28, besides teaching the course for critic teachers, Hulda taught two others. One was an upper-level curriculum course for elementary grades that focused on principles for selection and organization of curriculum for grades 1 through 6. The other course, Psychology of Childhood, was listed in the psychology and pedagogy section of the curriculum.

COLLEAGUE AND FRIEND

By 1927 Hulda and her colleague Professor Alberta Munkres had become the major faculty responsible for elementary education courses in the religious education section of the curriculum. They taught nine of the thirteen courses offered.

Their relationship began as teacher-student when Hulda entered Boston University. Hulda may have studied with Munkres in the course Principles of Elementary Work, which she took in her first year of study in 1919–20. Hulda probably worked closely with Munkres in the weekday demonstration school of which Hulda became director in 1922. Hulda mentioned that while continuing her studies, teaching as an assistant professor of the faculty, and directing the demonstration school, she also served as a substitute for the head of the elementary department "during her prolonged illness."[37]

There are two poems in Hulda's collection of "verse and doggerel" written for Alberta Munkres. This one has the notation, "For A.M.—the day before operation."

And He Stood Over Her
Luke 4:39

"They besought him for her,
And he stood over her,
And he rebuked the fever and it left her,
And she arose
And ministered to them."

Though that was long ago
And very far away
I read the record, over and again:
"They besought him for her
And he stood over her,
And he rebuked the fever and it left her,
And she arose
And ministered to them."

"They besought him for her,"
Is true today
"And he rebuked the fever,"
Of body and of soul
Is true today.
It must be also true today:
"And he stood over her," with healing in his presence.

So I read it over to my comfort:
"They besought him for her
And he stood over her,
And he rebuked the fever and it left her,
And she arose
And ministered to them."[38]

The feeling the poem communicates is one of warmth, care, and concern for a friend who was ill. It is consistent with her faith tradition experienced in the Niebuhr family that Hulda would recall a scripture passage and use it as a way not only to express care for Alberta but also to deal with her fear about her friend's health. Obvious in this poem is a statement of faith in God and God's healing powers.

Another poem, "The Fairy Ship," is noted as "written for Miss Munkres, March 4, 1924, 1st year Malden Supervisor." Malden was one of the sites used for demonstration and observation of teaching by the demonstration school. A portion of this poem gives indication of some of Hulda's concerns as a teacher. She used the image of a train to describe the adventure of teaching and learning.

The Train

Sometimes it starts me on a journey
At the end of which
I expect to see six visitors
Who want me to tell them
In three minutes,
While They wait to catch the
Next Train,
Just how to establish,
Run,
Budget
Curriculuate,
And man, (I mean woman)

> A School as much as possible
> Like our "Model."
> And when I arrive, Lo!—
> Not a soul is expecting me—
> All is peace and serenity.[39]

In addition to working with students who were preparing to be teachers, Hulda was responsible for teaching children in the classroom. The skill in striking the balance between teaching children, teaching adults, and administering this program is obvious when she writes:

> Sometimes, when the day has been going
> At such an even tenor
> That it seems
> A monotone,
> And I think
> "This day will have no fortissimos and crescendos"—
> Then the train takes me to a place
> Where there are two little Red Radicals,
> With all their redness
> Apparent,
> And a visitor who does not believe
> That you can teach little children
> Anything
> They want to know
> At that time of day,
> And a janitor
> Who is not present
> Because he is afflicted with
> Lumbago.[40]

At the end of a typed version of the poem found among the pages of the book of poetry is the notation, "Written for Miss Munkres' entertainment, Mar. 6, 1924. Hulda Niebuhr."[41]

In 1935, in the dedication page of her book *Ventures in Dramatics*, the inscription reads, "Dedicated to my Erstwhile Teacher, Alberta Munkres and to my Co-workers in the Madison Avenue Presbyterian Church, New York."[42] The formality of a teacher-student relationship, Miss Munkres and Miss Niebuhr, had been replaced by the warmth and familiarity of a relationship based on first names.

Alberta Munkres' book *Which Way For Our Children?* gives indication of her theory of religious education for children. In the first chapter,

"Inviting to the Search," she identified two approaches to working with children that parallel George Albert Coe's description of transmissive education and creative education. The latter she describes as one of inquiry using the experience of children. In this aspect, she echoed the concerns of Sophia Fahs, who she thanked in the preface for reading and commenting on her manuscript.[43]

Munkres' instruction in "Using the Bible with Children" gives clues about why she and Hulda felt a strong sense of colleagueship. They shared similar concerns for both the content and the application of biblical material.

> The Bible contains the traditions of Judaism and Christianity of which no one can afford to be ignorant, from the standpoint of literary merit or spiritual values. How and when can we best help children to experience these traditions vicariously so that they will not only sense man's quest for God in olden times in far-away Palestine, but may be inspired to continue that search today in the world in which they live?[44]

Munkres had a concern for helping children with the realities of life experiences, such as dealing with death and understanding social relationships, as well as their life in worship in the church. She demonstrates, along with Hulda, how religious educators were attempting to integrate a developmental understanding of children with what would later be called neoorthodox theology.

CHARACTER OF A LIFE

The School of Religious Education and Social Service of Boston University published a yearbook, *To Phos*, during the years when Hulda was a student. A picture of Hulda in this yearbook helps to continue developing the tapestry of her life. It is revealing in its description of her field and how her contribution was perceived by the students in this program. In the 1925 yearbook, her picture appears in the faculty section. Under her picture and field, elementary education, is this quotation: "Would you learn the ways of childhood— / Learn with them their songs and play? / Follow in Miss Niebuhr's footsteps, / She will show you childhood's way."[45]

The ten years Hulda lived in Boston evidence a very busy and fulfilling time in her life. Besides her responsibilities as a teacher, director of the weekday school, and a student, she was also engaged in writing. Hulda's book of poetry collected as a gift for her mother for Christmas 1929 is a revealing document, providing a way to understand some of the textures and colors of threads that wove together Hulda's life and work. The collection of poems is divided into four sections. The first is a collection of short poems "for Cynthia and other rhymes for children." Cynthia was Hulda's niece, the daughter of her brother H. Richard and his wife, Florence. The second section, entitled "Occasional Rhymes and Other 'Occasionals,'" contained, among others, "The Train," "To a Friend, Ill," and "Spirit of the Home." "So Much To Do" is one of the poems in the third section, entitled "Didactic Verse." The last section is named "Contemplations."

The person revealed in these poems is one of imagination and creativity, one who loved children. "My Daddy Can Fix It" is a representative poem.

My Daddy Can Fix It!

A doll is shattered—
But never a fear—
"My Daddy can fix it!"
A toy is battered—
But never a tear—
"My Daddy can fix it!"
How could it have mattered
When Daddy is near,
He's just at the office
And soon he'll be here—
Of course, then
"My Daddy will fix it!"[46]

The poem has this inscription at the end, "Cynthia—summer 1925." Hulda gives evidence of her close family ties and the love, support, and challenge she experienced in that setting.

Hulda also reveals the activity in her life and the demand and expectations she placed on herself. Though an introverted person, she lived life in relationship with friends and family and obviously enjoyed being with people. A real sense of whimsy and humor are revealed in some of her poems, as well as a delight in childhood and an understanding of developmental growth. Two poems, "Thanksgiving" and "Titles," indicate that Hulda was more interested in people knowing her as a real human being than in formal, titled ways. Her shy personality could have masked some of the warmth and genuineness within her.

Hulda's poem "Titles" was subtitled, "To a friend who will address me as 'Miss.'" In the poem Hulda struggled with labels.

I have been in assemblies of labelled prestiges
And have wished to be where one's name is just "comrade."
But I do not live in the Soviet Union
And really like the world I do live in.
"Comrade," after all, can be merely a title
And a formal label like your friend's name for you.
So—it is not really a matter, of great importance
What your friend calls you,
If you can hear when he calls
and understand what he tells you afterward.[47]

Beyond personal interaction, Hulda worked intentionally to understand the relationship between her faith and its practice in daily life. In 1925, her brother Reinhold had begun to make public statements about race in response to the rise of Klan activity in postwar Detroit. At that time migration of African-Americans from the South had increased from 5,700 in 1910 to 81,000 in 1925.[48]

In a country that was becoming increasingly polarized in terms of attitudes toward persons who were perceived as different from the norm of white Protestants, Hulda's experience in the church of her birth had prepared her for leadership that was desperately needed in offering a vision for what it meant to be Christian. Hulda's poem "Two Choirs" reveals her own understandings and commitments at this tense moment in the history of race relations in the United States. It also offers a glimpse into Hulda's deeply held beliefs about the value and worth of all people in the world. Such beliefs were foundational to her emerging philosophy of religious education.

Two Choirs

The one in Harlem—choir of brown-skinned boys,
Sedately surpliced, and with white-starched collars
Their boyishness subdued by reverence
Of time and place, veiled by the golden glow
Of candles, and enveloped in the radiance
Of jewelled high-arched windows flaming there.
Just once exchange of elfin, impish glance,
(Perhaps to prove that these were really boys
and not Grandmother's dream or artist's fancy
Of little boys) escaped from sparkling eyes
As quickly riveted again upon the notes.
They sang: "He is one God and he has made us,
Our God has made us and not we ourselves.
We are his sheep, the sheep of his own pasture.
Glory be to God, Most High."

And as they sang the reverent pews assented:
"Our God has made us and not we ourselves,—
Grant that in humble pride we may remember
We are thy children, thine elect, thine own."
"Across the line"—sons of the "lily white"
Sedately surpliced, and with white-starched collars
Their boyishness subdued by reverence
Of time and place, veiled by the golden glow
Of candles, and enveloped in the radiance
Of jeweled high-arched windows flaming there.
Just once a nudging elbow, paid by nudge,
(Perhaps to prove that these were really boys
And not Grandmother's dream or artist's fancy
Of little boys) broke through restraining bonds
As quickly to subside into demureness.[49]

Hulda's struggle with her calling as a Christian is obvious in her poem "Tinkling Cymbal."

Tinkling Cymbal

"Walk Jesus' path!" I preached, "And if it lead you—
To Calvary, what matter? Do as he!"
But while I walked his path and—theirs in fancy
I stood and looked beyond my Calvary.

And did not see the path that I should journey.
And did not see the needs there beckoning me.
I followed him, I thought. It was in fancy.
My feet had stayed while fancy wandered free.

Let me not say, "Go, follow Him," to others
til fancy shall no more my feet betray;
I will not teach, "His way of life is lovely"
Until my feet have walked in Jesus' way.[50]

It is possible that Hulda's poetry inspired her to write a book of stories for children. Perhaps it was also her association with Alberta Munkres. Munkres' book *I Wonder—Stories for Little Children* was published by Abingdon Press in 1930. It included one of Hulda's poems, "Try One," from her collection of poetry. In 1931, Charles Scribner's and Sons published Hulda's collection of stories for children, *Greatness Passing By*. Hulda must have been writing and collecting these stories for a number of years. She was also busy writing curriculum for use in the Sunday school at Bethel

Church in Detroit. A member of the church wrote, "Hulda Niebuhr was attending Boston University at this time. She was working on new church school materials. She would send copies to Mother Niebuhr and our church school staff would put it in motion. What a wonderful opportunity for our School."[51]

THE DEVELOPING TEACHER

In 1927 at age thirty-eight, Hulda was one of three women assistant professors on the faculty of the School of Religious Education and Social Service. There were three women with the title of professor and ten listed as instructor. Out of a faculty of forty-five, twenty-nine were males. Of these, six were instructors, three were assistant professors, and twenty were professors. Fields dominated by women included education, religious education, drama, and psychology. Three women were employed as teachers of English, Italian, and English Bible.

Her administrative abilities as director of the weekday demonstration school had been developed in her previous work with her father, her mother, and her brother Reinhold. Her leadership, however, was distinguished from that of her mother. Hulda, though tied closely to her family emotionally, was able to establish her identity and authority in claiming her vocation as an educator. She was not tied to a family member for her self-identity or self-development.

At this time Hulda also developed her self-understanding as a religious educator and began to live out that definition. Previously, she had seen herself as a practitioner. Her experiences at Bethel Evangelical Church and her studies and teaching at Boston University achieved what Athearn's philosophy had intended, a grounding and blending of theory and practice.

Hulda's understanding of the vocation of religious educator was implicit in her book of children's stories, *Greatness Passing By*. It articulates an important concept in her theory of religious education: the appropriateness of teaching methods related to the age and experience of the learner. The book also provided Hulda with the chance to experiment with her gifts as a writer of children's stories, an activity that she used extensively in her teaching at McCormick Theological Seminary. In the preface to the book, Hulda describes the power of the story.

The magic of the story's words causes the imagination of each hearer to work in an original, creative fashion even though the general pattern is indicated, for each imagination paints its screen with the pigments and shapes of its own interpretation, out of its own background of experience. Although they come out of the background of personal experience these pictures constitute a new world. They open the door to new experience. The story takes the hearer out of his present-day world into a new realm of new associations and sets him watching in curiosity for the next development.[52]

She contrasts the power of this magic and its ability to engage the learner with the negative capacities as used by some teachers whose intent is to tell students what they should learn from the story.

That is, instead of constructing and telling a story which may make its own direct appeal to the hearer, the teller surcharges his material with the feeling he himself has about the facts or truths or persons involved. The sweetly sentimental stories about Jesus, for instance, found in so much children's literature, often cause an aftermath of revulsion against the counterfeit emotion they called forth, when more realistic stories might have generated soundly based and enduring appreciations.[53]

These convictions about the relationship between the method of teaching and the learner were foundational in Hulda's emerging philosophy of religious education. This concept is also obvious in her poem "What Some of Them Said," written as if the walls of classrooms were telling stories about the kind of teaching that went on within them. She contrasts walls of rooms that are uncared for, rooms with bare walls, walls covered with material irrelevant to the topic or age group, and walls that "talked too much" with what she believed was the best kind of primary room.

> These sunny walls, in quiet voice
> Through pictures of a thoughtful choice
> Spoke of the loving care of Mother,
> Said, "Be ye kind to one another"
> "Theirs is the kingdom, let them come,"
> Just that. Add on the burlap some
> Few pictures chosen for the day
> Because harmoniously they say
> One helpful thing for children's ears
> To be remembered through the years.
> In accents worthy of the place
> These walls helped children grow in grace.
> They spoke with *authority*![54]

If Hulda had gone to Boston with the intention of claiming a theory to support her practice of religious education, she succeeded in that goal. She was able to leave Boston University having established her identity separate from her family; she established her reputation as a teacher and developed as a creative, intelligent, and caring woman.

Clockwise from left: Lydia, Walter, Hulda, and Walter's daughter
Carol in Knoxville, Tennessee, 1935

3

A Vocational Transformation (1928–1945)

IF PHOTOGRAPHS EXISTED for this period of Hulda Niebuhr's life, they probably would provide glimpses into two interrelated areas of her life. One photograph might capture her life in the apartment she shared with her mother, showing Hulda working at her typewriter on a paper for class, a journal article, or a manuscript for a book. Another picture would capture the afternoon teas that junior high girls from Madison Avenue Presbyterian Church were invited to share with Hulda and Lydia or teaching students representing a variety of careers and theological backgrounds in a class in religious education at New York University.

It would be hard to illustrate Hulda's life within the institution of Madison Avenue Presbyterian Church with just one photograph. A video camera that could have followed her around the church, the neighborhood, and the city would have been a more appropriate way to capture the nature of Hulda's ministry and educational leadership within the church, the university, and the community, since its locus was much broader than the buildings occupied by the church.

In describing the transition from Boston to New York, Hulda said that she was interested in getting perspective because

> always while teaching I felt I was telling more than I knew, that religious education theory hung on slender threads, that I must get perspective on our work in Boston, so I took a year's leave of absence to study in Union Seminary and Teacher's College of Columbia, with the intention of taking a Ph.D. should I decide to stay within academic work.[1]

The period of 1928 to 1930 must have been a time of reflection, vocational assessment, and personal evaluation as she moved to New York City to live with her mother and her brother Reinhold. As she survived the transition from faculty member at Boston University to graduate student in the doctoral program of Union Theological Seminary and Columbia University, she also struggled with a career decision.

Hulda had chosen the field of religious education for her vocation. Until this point, her experience working as a religious educator had been limited to churches where her father and her brother Reinhold had been called as pastors. A letter that Hulda wrote to the president of McCormick Theological Seminary in 1945 suggests the vocational struggle in which she was involved.

> Because of my interest in interracial problems there had been some pressure upon me to teach in some Negro institution and I was weighing that possibility. However, my race-conscious Negro friends helped me to decide against that, and also my further year in academic environment made me surer than ever that I wanted to work at religious education before I did any more talking about it.[2]

Madison Avenue Presbyterian Church offered Hulda the opportunity to put her theory into practice. This period of her life also allowed her to test her assumptions by teaching courses in religious education at New York University. Finally, she was able to produce her greatest amount of writing, focusing on the practical application of teaching methods in the church.

LEAVING AND TRANSITION

Hulda needed to separate herself both from what she had been learning and what she had been teaching in order to reflect on their meaning. Separation meant to her both physical and philosophical distance. She chose to take a year's leave of absence from her position as a faculty member in the School of Religious Education and Social Service of Boston University in 1928–29, move to New York City, and enroll in the doctoral program at Union Seminary and Columbia University. The goals of her outward journey were obvious.

Identifying Hulda's inward journey helps to complete the picture of this transitional time in her life, one both of reflection and vocational assessment. Her decision to leave Boston must be placed in the larger context of her education, her career, and her family. Hulda's dissertation was completed during the first semester of the 1927–28 school year and graduation took place June 18, 1928. The Boston University Bulletin for 1928–30 lists Hulda Niebuhr, assistant professor of elementary education in the School of Religious Education and Social Service, and indicated she would be on a leave of absence for 1928–29.[3] Such leave had to have been requested early in the second semester of 1928.

Other members of her family were also in transition. It is important to consider Hulda's decisions in light of this familial context. Reinhold's fame and reputation were growing because of his frequent public speaking engagements and the publication of his books. He was approached in the fall of 1927 about a part-time teaching position at Union Seminary. Reinhold had previously turned down an offer to teach at Boston University. The appointment to Union was accepted and became public April 1928, when he announced he was leaving Bethel Church in Detroit. In 1930, Reinhold first met Ursula Keppel-Compton, an English fellow studying for a year at Union Seminary. They married in England in December 1931.

H. Richard Niebuhr at this time had begun serving as academic dean at Eden Seminary, a position he held until 1931, when he joined the faculty at Yale Divinity School. Walter had returned from Europe after the war and was receiving financial support from Reinhold as he attempted to rebuild his career in filmmaking. Lydia was living with Reinhold in Detroit, where her life was focused on maintaining the day-to-day administration of Reinhold's household and Bethel Church.

Between 1927 and 1930, several significant individual and familial transitions were taking place that help to explain the responses of family members. The family, though spread out, seems to have been a very close one. Reinhold had assumed responsibility for his mother and his siblings. When considering the decision to leave Detroit he mentioned, "my personal problem still demands my leaving."[4] Richard Fox speculates whether the problem was a relationship with a woman, the need to claim finally personal independence from his mother, or the need for increased income to support his brother and mother.[5] In considering the family situation, the latter two options seem more likely to have been a motivating factor for the move.

It was probably a combination of personal and vocational reasons that were the major factors in Reinhold's decision to move to New York. He must have known that the move would have profound effects on his mother. Tied so closely for her identity and self-development as a paraprofessional in the church, Lydia was facing for the first time a life without a congregational role as "assistant pastor." It was a role she had assumed for over forty years.

What normally would appear as a fairly simple vocational decision for a young man gifted as a preacher, teacher, public speaker, and spiritual leader took on much greater proportions considering the personal and professional relationships he shared with his mother. Reinhold had replaced his father in terms of the responsibility for his mother's life and emotional health. In describing Lydia's health, Fox has said, "She was subject to periodic bouts of anxiety, and heavily dependent on Bethel Church for equilibrium."[6] After the move to New York:

> Lydia, still an energetic woman as she passed her sixtieth birthday in December, 1929, was despondent, languishing in idleness. She was depressed by her lack of productivity, by the drain she exerted on her son's pocketbook, but most of all by the end of her partnership with him in the work of the Lord. She could not help feeling abandoned.[7]

The implication of these statements is the picture of a woman still bound culturally to a traditional woman's role of duplicating her husband emotionally and, in this case, professionally. From her adolescence, Lydia's role as pastoral assistant had enabled her father, her husband, and her son Reinhold to experience the success of public professional careers. Lydia seemed to achieve self-identity and self-development through her support of her family members, allowing her own achievements to serve as a necessary background for their accomplishments. Lydia's own identity as an individual and as a professional religious educator was never understood separate from the pastoral roles of her father, her husband, and her son.

The move to New York City represented for Lydia a real time of disequilibrium—both personally and professionally. She was no longer needed to run the church. For the first time in her life she was not moving to another church.

When her function as housekeeper was no longer necessary because of Reinhold's marriage to Ursula, Lydia experienced the ultimate separation. Fox has commented on the implication of Reinhold's marriage. "He was not just leaving his childhood home; for Lydia at least it was abandonment, if not desertion, divorce, and remarriage."[8]

Hulda could not have been unaware of the implications of Reinhold's move. His conversation with Union Seminary president Henry Sloane Coffin had begun in the fall of 1927, at a time when Hulda was completing her master's thesis. She must also have been considering her own vocational future. A major part of her educational work had focused on religious education.

Hulda needed perspective on Athearn's zealous plan for religious education and its partnership with local communities for the growth in faith of its children. Perhaps she also was aware of the financial situation of the School of Religious Education and Social Service and wondered what changes would be enacted with a new dean in place. Her place as teacher in the weekday program could well have been a tenuous one with the departure of Athearn. She was most likely seeking perspective on the religious education that she had experienced and practiced with her father and mother, the theology taught and lived in the Niebuhr home, in contrast to the education she had received at Boston University.

A PERSONAL TRANSFORMATION

The move to New York City was pivotal personally to Hulda because it meant taking both unknown as well as familiar steps. At an age when a majority of women of her generation were focused on family and children or trying to balance their lives at home with their careers, their futures fairly clearly laid out before them, Hulda experienced the difficult transition from professor to doctoral student. Her future was open, only possibilities could be imagined. The steps were familiar in that she moved home, at a time of transition, of questioning, of even depression, home to mother where each could care for the other.

Hulda chose to detach herself from an institution to which she had been subordinated and to begin to ask questions. She had to choose to individuate, to choose not just to move home and care for her mother but to enter a doctoral program where she would have the resources available to help her "get perspective on our work in Boston."

After moving to New York, probably during the summer of 1928, Hulda was admitted to graduate study in September 1928 for the doctor of philosophy in education in the joint program of Teacher's College of Columbia University and Union Theological Seminary. She studied in that program for two years through the winter session of 1930.[9]

The doctoral program that she chose offered her the breadth of knowledge from the two schools. It was a self-directed program with no specific course requirements or proportions of classes to be taken in the two schools. A student having selected a major interest and a major professor would participate in a joint advisory system consisting of faculty from both schools. It was estimated that at least three years of academic study, including thirty points of course work and dissertation preparation, would be required to complete the necessary degree requirements.[10]

In her first year of study, 1928–29, Hulda completed five courses, focusing on human development, curriculum, and research methods, in the education department at Teacher's College. In her studies at Columbia with Harold Rugg and William Heard Kilpatrick, she continued the focus on elementary-age children that she had initiated at Boston University.

During the 1929–30 winter session, Hulda was registered for six courses, three in each school. At Teacher's College, she continued her studies with Rugg in a course in social psychology and a course in methods of research with James Ralph McGaughy. She added a course in the philosophy of education.

At Union, she took two courses in psychology, Personality Difficulties and Psychology of Personality, both taught by Harrison Sacket Elliott, and a third, Educational Approach to Christian Professional Leadership. This latter course was team-taught by Elliott, Erdman Harris, Sophia Lyon Fahs, and Frank Wilbur Herriott. Her transcript shows that she was absent from the final exam in the philosophy of education course and received an incomplete in the research methods course. No grade appears at all for the course in Educational Approach to Leadership.

If she had completed her course work, she would have had the requisite minimum of thirty points needed for the course requirements in the doctoral program. The obvious question is why did she fail to complete three of her courses? The only clues come from Hulda and her brother H. Richard. Her poem "Rap-a-Tap," dated June 1929, indicates she was hospitalized for a period of time. Whether it was for her chronic back problem or for her emotional health is unknown.

In the poem she describes the various people who "rap" at her hospital door, friends, family, and medical personnel. What she communicates in this poem is the care and warmth that she needed and that she received while she was "prone in a hospital bed." The poem ends with these words, "the raps at my door keep my spirit tip-toe / Though I'm prone in a hospital bed."[11]

In a letter found in Hulda's book of poetry, *This and That*, a friend from Boston shares her comments on some of Hulda's poetry. Her friend concludes her letter: "I hope it is being an intensely interesting year for you, and that you are satisfactorily escaping the clutches of the psychologists."[12]

One other factor that could be understood as a contributor to her emotional health at this time was an experience of unrequited love. Hulda fell in love with someone famous, a colleague at work, someone well known, and was extremely loyal to him. Her niece, Carol Buchanan, describes this time as "just a sadness" in Hulda's life, since the man she loved married someone else.[13]

Perhaps her hospitalization prevented Hulda from completing her course work. This also could have been the time of her depression, to which she was periodically subject, a pivotal time when she succumbed to her own weaknesses and emotional needs, brought on perhaps by the loss of her love, the anguish of her mother, the displacement of the move from Boston, and the struggle to name and claim her voice and integrity in competition with the requirements and expectations of a graduate faculty.

Hulda's emotional health was obvious to H. Richard, who reported the advice he had given to Hulda in a letter he wrote to Reinhold. H. Richard told Hulda that

> we were all inclined to introversion, and that it wasn't a good plan to introspect too much when we got into some psychical difficulty, because we found too many symptoms, and thought ourselves to be suffering from lots of things which were after all nothing but formal manifestations.[14]

He went on to say that he thought the difficulties she was experiencing were normal. His advice on dealing with such complexities was "to get busy on something external, preferably something manual."[15]

The degree of Hulda's emotional difficulties during this period of her life is hard to measure. In one of her "Letters to a Dear but Departed Spouse," Ursula Neibuhr remembered this time in Hulda's life.

> I had my suspicions about the family all being peace and love. After all, your brother had two very bad nervous crack-ups. Your sister also did, just about the time we became "involved" and engaged. I remember you getting off the boat at Southampton when you came over to visit my family in 1931 and telling me, "Our future happiness depends on the frail thread of my sister's health."[16]

Publicly she made clear her reasons for not completing the doctoral degree.

> I had done most of the work needed for a Ph.D. except the dissertation, but Teacher's College was in an era when everything had to be proven by questionnaires and I was not interested in taking a good year out of my life to work on anything that suggested itself within the limitations. Besides I had decided upon practical work in the church and I never gathered up my credits.[17]

In her doctoral work at Union Seminary and Teacher's College, Hulda found the courses she needed to further her education. Her reflections on this time of graduate study indicate that what was important to her was how the course work could satisfy her needs. Meeting degree requirements was not a priority.

In courses at Union and Teacher's College Hulda encountered progressive education as it had been interpreted by educators after John Dewey. Rugg's and Shumaker's *The Child Centered School* recognized children as artists and recognized the power of schools to foster their creativity. Hulda also encountered William Heard Kilpatrick, a student of Dewey's, who was concerned with learning as a purposeful activity within a social environment.[18]

Though Harrison Elliott carried on Coe's tradition at Union Seminary, his narrow focus on group process and his rigid adherence to liberal theology made him somewhat of an anomaly by the late 1940s. Sophia Fahs was also a student of Coe, Hugh Hartshorne, and Edward Lee Thorndike and was concerned with appropriate teaching methods that would strengthen the religious education of children. What was important to Fahs was how children learned, how their experiences were used to help build their faith, and the value of learning from world religions.[19]

It is possible to draw several conclusions about the influences that the educational institutions in Boston and New York had on Hulda's emerging theory of religious education. Such influences must be understood in light of Hulda's theological and educational formation within the Niebuhr family.

Hulda took with her to Boston a clear understanding of a Christocentric theology. It is no wonder that she found a welcome home theologically with Walter Athearn's School of Religious Education and Social Service at Boston University. Hulda also shared Athearn's vision of the broad impact of religious education in helping to nurture individuals in faithful Christian living. With Alberta Munkres at Boston University and Sophia Fahs at Union Theological Seminary Hulda shared a developmental understanding of children and the importance of using teaching methods appropriate to the age of the learner.

Hulda was thirty-nine when she began her doctoral studies, far from being an impressionable, young graduate student. She was probably less influenced by the theological perspective at Union/Columbia than she was by the educational philosophy. It is more correct to say that Hulda found compatibility with some of the major tenets of progressive education, particularly in the emphasis on the creativity inherent in children and the role of the teaching and learning environment in fostering that creativity.

The educational institutions in which Hulda studied offered her the opportunity to confirm important educational and theological assumptions that she had experienced in the Niebuhr home and in her educational work in churches in Lincoln, Illinois, and Detroit, Michigan. Her studies in those schools all furthered her continuing transformation from student to educational leader.

The transition of Hulda's inward journey involved coming to terms with her status as a single woman and claiming her identity distinct from her mother. Since H. Richard Niebuhr destroyed all his correspondence with Hulda after her death, it is impossible to know what he said to her during this time. What is possible to know is that Hulda did proceed to "get busy on something external." Within the next six years she had accepted a job at Madison Avenue Presbyterian Church, written two books, and begun teaching as a lecturer at New York University. These years of transition and development were ones where Hulda was able to assess her past and to begin to plan for her future in her career as church educator and professor.

A VOCATIONAL TRANSFORMATION

Hulda went to New York and to Madison Avenue Presbyterian Church in 1930 seeking answers for her vocational questions and her concerns about the field of religious education and the theories on which it was based. The September 9, 1930, edition of *The Weekly*, the newsletter of the Madison Avenue Presbyterian Church, announced that Hulda Niebuhr, "with a long record of study and preparation and wide experience in leadership," joined the staff as a part-time worker.[20] The church was excited about her expertise in religion and the arts and believed it would be "an intensely valuable pioneering effort."[21]

The announcement of Hulda's employment with the church gave few details of what her job would entail, other than using her expertise in the communication of religion through the arts. Fine arts were her entry into the life and work of a congregation that had a strong commitment to liturgy, education, and the arts—music, visual arts, and drama. Though her work began as a part-time position with special emphasis on the approach to religion through the arts, by 1941 it had evolved into a position as associate director of religious education, including partial supervision of four assistant directors of religious education.

Her official duties as listed in the announcement of her departure in 1945 included:

the selection, creation and coordination of curriculum materials, the choosing, training and coaching of teachers, the direction of the Intermediate and Senior Departments of the Church School, the guidance of the worship experience of Juniors, Intermediates and Seniors, and the supervision of week-day activities for Junior and Senior High School pupils.[22]

This can be understood as no small task in a church of several thousand members. A listing of the staff in 1944 includes, in addition to Hulda's position, three ministers, a church executive, an organist and choir director, an assistant organist and director of youth choirs, four assistant directors of religious education, nine student seminary assistants, and seven members of the maintenance staff.

In her letter to Harry Cotton, president of McCormick, she said that in her work at the church, "I have been given great freedom to do here what I thought was important."[23] Administration, teaching, writing, and designing educational programs were large parts of what she thought was important.

The years Hulda spent at Madison Avenue Presbyterian Church, from 1930 to 1945, gave her the time and place to test her theory of religious education. The "great freedom" that she was given is illustrated in two dimensions of her work. The church provided her with freedom to design and implement a program of religious education for children and youth. And by teaching as a lecturer in religious education at New York University from 1938 to 1946, she had the freedom to test her assumptions.

During this time she wrote two books; translated another book from German into English with her sister-in-law, Barbara Keppel-Compton, Ursula Niebuhr's sister; and wrote four articles for *The International Journal of Religious Education*. These fifteen years represent years of several different kinds of freedom for self-expression that served to confirm the direction and the scope of her continuing development as a professional woman.

The last sentence of the article announcing Hulda's employment at Madison Avenue Presbyterian Church suggests how difficult it must have been for her to achieve her own identity. "Of interest is the fact that she is a sister of Reinhold Niebuhr and of Richard Niebuhr, and the fact that her mother is one of the teachers in our Junior Department."[24] As a professional woman in a notable family, it was difficult for Hulda to be recognized for who she was or for what she had accomplished as an individual. Hulda joined Madison Avenue Presbyterian Church as a member on September 1, 1931.And apparently Lydia Niebuhr had not wasted much time in finding a new church and becoming involved as a leader either.[25]

Hulda began her work at the church with a focus on the arts and religious education; however, the focus of her time shifted to working with "juniors," young people between the ages of ten and fifteen.

Hulda had many opportunities to work with juniors directly in teaching and learning activities in the church school, in planning with them for their Sunday morning service of worship, and in administering their weekday activities. She also developed and taught in programs of leadership training for adults who were working with this age group.

An examination of church newsletters and her writing reveals Hulda's working philosophy of religious education. Also evident is a well-articulated explanation of two teaching/learning methods, drama and storytelling, that she used extensively and the appropriateness of these methods in relation to children and younger youth and their developmental needs. Revealed in her writing is a theological basis for her philosophy that serves as a goal toward which she believed religious educators must work. To understand this philosophy, it is essential to place it in the context of Madison Avenue Presbyterian Church.

"A CHURCH OUGHT NOT TO BE CHRISTIAN AT ARM'S LENGTH"

Madison Avenue Presbyterian was a church on a journey, seeking to establish itself as a leader among Protestant denominations in the city of New York. It was also a congregation committed to helping its members develop as mature and responsible Christians in society. Founded in 1835, "with its wide service to all classes to people," Madison Avenue Presbyterian Church demonstrated how one congregation sought to respond to issues of the day by confronting its members with Christianity concerned with transformation of the culture, not cultural accommodation.[26] A survey of church newsletter articles during the years of Hulda Niebuhr's employment, 1930 to 1945, gives evidence of the church's vision for Christian leadership.

As a congregation, it was concerned both with ministry within the institution and within the community. Articles from the *Madison Avenue Presbyterian Church News* reveal a concern for the family and the many changes it was facing in a rapidly shifting culture. Articles on divorce, movies and their impact on children, ways to observe the Sabbath, and the importance of religious education in the home were predominant. Equally important was the encouragement of members and their responsibilities as Christians in a democratic society. Articles on voter registration, the child labor amendment, a living wage for apparel workers, and a plea for clothes and jobs for unemployed men were in evidence during the 1930s.[27] The women's movement did not go unaddressed by the church. In 1932, an article reported women in elected leadership positions in Presbyterian churches at a time when the denomination continued to refuse to ordain women as ministers. In 1936, an article addressed the issue of a minimum wage law for women.

World peace was an important concern beginning in the early 1930s and continuing until the involvement of the United States in World War II. "The Next War, Should the Church Support It?" in 1931, "The Church Looks Toward Peace," and the announcement of the establishment of a peace library in the church in 1938 show the concern of the leadership of this congregation. Another continuing social issue was race relations in the city. Several articles in the *Madison Avenue Presbyterian Church News* gave examples of how the church worked within its programs of religious education and its activities in social ministry to help its members become involved in face-to-face activities with many of the ethnic groups within the city.

Before combining with the Phillips Church at 53rd and Madison Avenue in New York City in 1899, Madison Avenue Church had experienced several moves, mergers, and name changes since its formation in 1835. The facilities at the time of Hulda Niebuhr's employment included a sanctuary, the Phillips Chapel, and a church house that had space for classes, meetings, club activities, offices, a gym, bowling alley, swimming pool, residences, and a covered roof garden. In a sermon preached May 14, 1939, George Buttrick commented that "now it seems too small at times, but then [1916] it was a great venture of faith: people asked, 'whoever heard of a church needing a ten-story Church house?'"[28]

A rich diversity of ethnic backgrounds contributed to its membership. Originally Scottish and English groups were dominant. Later immigrants from other parts of Europe joined the church. In the latter part of the nineteenth century, Hungarians and Czechoslovakians were welcomed as they sought to escape revolutions in their countries. In 1939, the church had 2,857 members and a budget of $155,000. It was the largest Presbyterian church in New York City.

In a brief history written for its 150th anniversary, five aspects of the congregation's ministry were highlighted. A first commitment to Christian education had always been a priority. "Early at Madison and 73rd Street, about fifty people attended church school and Bible classes: in 1939, that number rose to 1,150."[29] The first vacation Bible school in New York City was begun at Madison Avenue in the early 1900s. The church was considered to be a place of learning for members as well as for seminarians "numbering in the hundreds over the years, [who] have both contributed to and grown from the educational opportunities at Madison Avenue Presbyterian Church."[30]

The music program, a second commitment at the church, not only enriched their public worship during this era, it also provided connections with the community through concerts, both instrumental and choral. Music was also a source of rich ecumenicity in the sharing of varieties of musical traditions among denominations, races, and ethnic groups in New York City. It is not difficult to imagine the impact of this ministry when considering the growth of the city during this time and the impact of large immigrant groups moving in and among the longer term residents.

The third commitment to "neighborhood ministry" describes the core of the church's self-understanding. The church was established in 1835 as the Manhattan Island Church, a mission in "the swamp," which is the dry dock region of New York City today.[31] Operating out of a building whose upper floors had served as a Baptist mission and whose lower floor was a school, the church ministered "largely to the homes of workers in the shipyards built where the swamp creeks flowed into the East River."[32] More commonly and in keeping with its location, the mission was known as "The Church in the Swamp."

A fourth priority of Madison Avenue Presbyterian Church was financial support of community, national, and world missions. The church's relationship with mission work in China, Asia, and the Middle East was extensive. The congregation was involved in establishing a mission station and later a church in Nanhsuchow, China. In addition to a chapel, the mission included schools, a hospital with clinic and dispensary, and an agricultural experimental and training station for wheat production. Support for colleges and family service centers was also an important part of the church's relationship with Christians around the world.

Finally, the church never conceived of itself as ministering solely to its own members nor did it understand itself to be in partnership only with its own denomination. The sixth strong commitment of the church was to its community, its country, and to the world when called upon for response to crisis situations. When special needs arose, such as those growing out of the stock market crash and ensuing depression and World Wars I and II, the church responded financially, educationally, and through the sharing of human resources.

A life can be imagined as a tapestry with events, experiences, and relationships providing the varieties, colors, and textures of the cloth. In her letter to Harry Cotton, president of McCormick Theological Seminary, in their early correspondence about the possibility of her accepting a position on the faculty of the Presbyterian College of Christian Education, Hulda said that "Madison Avenue Church with its wide service to all classes of people had interested me and I was happy to take a position there."[33] What in this particular church's theology, practice of ministry, and programs of religious education attracted Hulda Niebuhr to take a position on its educational staff? What threads did the church offer to Hulda's tapestry of life and what chapters did she add to their faith story?

Madison Avenue Church, from its very beginning, sought to embody a theology that united faith in God and responsible activity in the world. In the late 1880s, after the move to Madison Avenue, the church started a goodwill branch on 51st Street between Second and Third Avenues so that children could attend Sunday school without the danger of crossing the railroad tracks. Separate facilities for study and worship were maintained until the pastorate of the Reverend Henry Sloane Coffin, which began in 1905.

Two long-standing hierarchical traditions were broken during his pastorate, which lasted until 1927. At one of the children's worship services in 1944, a statement, "This Is Our Church," told in the words of children what had caused one of these reforms.

> When Dr. Coffin first came, this church paid its bills with rents for the pews. The people who could pay the most had the best seats on Sunday morning and the people who could not pay anything had to sit on the sides or wait till the others were seated and take the seats that were left. The people of the church began to see that it was not Christian for people to have preference according to what they could afford and pew rents were done away with. Since then everyone can sit where he will and the bills of the church are paid by everyone doing the best he can to support the church.[34]

Threatening to resign if the Goodwill Mission was not merged with the church, Dr. Coffin was heard to say, "A church ought not to be Christian at arm's length."[35] Being Christian at this church meant critically examining its own practice of Christianity as much as critiquing the Christian's responsibility in the world.

Articles in the church's weekly newsletter, *The Weekly* and later *The Madison Avenue Presbyterian Church News*, provide glimpses into how the church nurtured its members in the Christian faith between 1930 and 1945. Worship and religious education were at the heart of the church's life. Services for children, church school for all ages, worship both Sunday morning and evening, and midweek schools for adults provided opportunities for biblical study and public worship, appropriately planned for each age group in the church.

"Growth through action" is an appropriate description of the expectation the church had of its members. Buttrick, in his historical sermon for the centennial celebration, described the commitment of his predecessor, Henry Sloan Coffin, to a "'church for all people' beyond all accidents of birth and class."[36] Buttrick's pastorate with the church lasted from 1927 to 1954. He followed in the tradition of Coffin in seeking to develop the social consciousness of the congregation through engagement with biblical teaching and preaching. For Buttrick, the intention of the church's beliefs and activities was essential.

> Let us not fail, either in preaching or friendship, to let it be known that in Christ there is grace for the sinner, comfort for the sorrowing, cheer for the depressed pilgrim, light for the baffled mind and all winsomeness for little children and all concern for the young.... Here let it be known through faith...that we obey the command of Christ, "Go into all the world." Let this church remain being a "Church for All People." Let it still be a part of practical endeavors, but let the Spirit of God animate all its works lest it should ever become a body without a soul. From Him came the original flame; He has been the passion of our journeying years; unto Him be our continuing and final zeal.[37]

Members of the church were nurtured, challenged, and supported in their Christian faith. In turn they were expected to remember their calling. When the church moved to its site on Fifty-fifth Street, the congregation did not have a pastor. The elders of the church prepared a message to the congregation as they moved into their new home. The members of the church that was to become Madison Avenue Presbyterian Church were reminded to "never forget that the vows of God are upon you, and that they will follow you wherever you go."[38]

To be a part of Madison Avenue Presbyterian Church meant that it was impossible to conceive of Christian consciousness and social consciousness as separate entities. Knowing and being were inextricably woven together, fibers of the same thread in the tapestry of Christian living.

EDUCATION NOT AT ARM'S LENGTH

Educational programs of the church were divided according to age. Hulda had specific responsibilities as superintendent of the intermediate department, which had an enrollment in 1936 of 228. As superintendent, her job would have consisted of recruiting, training, and supporting teachers for the seven girls' and nine boys' classes in this department of the Sunday school. It also meant that she supervised those who were in charge of this age group's weekday functions, which included club, gym, and swimming activities.

It becomes obvious that the supervision of even one children's department in the church involved administrative complexity far greater than that of some congregations. An article in *The Weekly* entitled, "Who's Who?" provided notes from the intermediate department to inform the congregation of its purpose and activities.

> The Intermediate Department has a "house of representatives" known as the Council, which consists of representatives of the sixteen classes and the department superintendent. This group manages much of the business of the department, such as appointment of classes to take charge of ushering in the worship service, the editing of the department periodical, "The Intermediate Scribble," planning of occasional parties and the annual hobby show, respectively, the delegation of such duties, and chiefly, the planning of the benevolence budget. Probably most of the Council's time is spent in stimulating the pupils of the department to interest themselves in the various items in the benevolent budget.[39]

This informative article ends with words of support for the vital relationships between the home and the church and encourages parents to take initiative, "for the interest of parents in prompt and regular attendance and in high standards of accomplishment is one of the prime requisites of really good church school work."[40]

Hulda's responsibilities with this age group were more than a task. She shared with her mother a love for children. In a letter she described some activities they provided for children of the church.

> Those youngsters, mostly from the over crowded homes which then obtained in East Side, were often in our apartment, serving each other Sunday luncheons, responsible by groups for different courses, or possibly slumber parties. Any trips of mine out of the city were signal for a looked for slumber party—then there was room in the apartment for more girls.[41]

Lydia had been provided a movie camera by her son Walter and had achieved a reputation as a filmmaker. Her topics were ones that would appeal to children, such as "Nature's Round," "Our Helpers." "That was in the days before TV and children's movies and Mother became known as a resource for settlement houses and vacation schools. So she travelled all over New York City with her projector in the early days there."[42] Lydia and Hulda's apartment was really an open house for the young people with whom they worked in the congregation. They believed that the context of learning in the home could be as important as what was learned in class. This philosophy continued to be important to Hulda with her students on the McCormick Theological Seminary campus.

Hulda's additional responsibilities at Madison Avenue Presbyterian Church are evident from articles appearing in the church newsletter. A conference for young women in 1931 had as its theme, "How Can I be a Christian in New York?" In addition to struggling with issues related to the economic situation, the participants were led in addressing personal issues of living the Christian life. "Miss Hulda Niebuhr led us on Saturday evening on the theme of finding God in the beautiful things of the world, and what a thrilling picture she painted."[43]

Hulda worked with children in writing plays that were frequently presented in the 9:30 A.M. Sunday church service. One of these plays, "Thanksgiving for Our Time," was described in an article for *The International Journal of Religious Education*. The process of writing those plays, if the article is any indication of norm, used an inductive teaching style beginning with questions, followed by study by the children, and then the actual writing of the play. The dramas dealt with issues of social consciousness, including race and working conditions, and with the enactment of biblical stories.

Teaching adults in the church was another major part of Hulda's responsibilities. A survey of newsletter articles reveals topics of sessions and courses that she taught during her years of employment. In the adult school of religion post-Easter session of 1936, Hulda spoke on "Christ in Recent Art," and the article notes that this was to be an illustrated presentation. In 1934, she led an adult discussion entitled "How I Can Teach Religion." The Lenten school for adults in 1944 included "Introduction to Bible Teaching" by Hulda. It was offered for teachers, persons interested in teaching, and parents. Topics to be considered were:

> the Bible as any enjoyable and exciting book for children and young people; the Bible as an indispensable book for children and young people; a survey of areas of understanding and knowledge in which the Bible teacher needs to be "at home"; principles any teacher needs to regard applied to Bible teaching; some common pitfalls; resources for the teacher of the Bible.[44]

In 1945, members of the educational staff, including Hulda, were involved in a discussion course for parents, "Answering Children's Questions About the Bible," focusing on different kinds of Bible literature, how and when the books of the Bible were written, the Bible as a holy book, "Changing concept of God in the Bible," "Dealing with difficult questions about—God, the cross, birth of Jesus," and resources to help parents.[45]

An important part of any church educator's job is the teaching and training of teachers for the church school. In 1940, Madison Avenue Church supported and participated in the Central Community School of Religion held at St. Nicholas Collegiate Church, a nearby congregation. Included in the list of courses was "How Do We Guide Children and Youth into Christian Living?" taught by Hulda Niebuhr and Lillian White Shepard. The course was designed for teachers and leaders who worked with youth, ages 9 to 16, and was planned to "help leaders discover how to proceed most effectively, considering the place of worship, study and discussion, service and other activities in a complete program."[46] In 1941, Hulda taught "Worship as Part of the Curriculum."

"Couldn't something be done to get parents to go to school so they could get over their discriminations?" was the question asked in "They All Believe in Charity," an article in the church newsletter. The title of another article, "Making a Better World," came from a discussion among the church's high school students and Rabbi Perilman of Temple Emanuel. The article concluded that "when our true desire is for the good of others, then all our relationships, as employee, employer, voter, citizen, traveller, customer, pupil, teacher, parent, friend, become channels of the Lord's mercy, and the world will necessarily be that much better."[47]

Obviously the monthly issues of the *Teacher's Bulletin* did not retreat from issues of the day. Consistent with the theology of the church, the educational program of Madison Avenue called learners of all ages into responsible discipleship and nurtured them for their faithful journeys. Hulda Niebuhr was a part of and a major contributor to the church and its "wide service to all classes of people." Her creativity during this period was obvious in the publication of two books and four articles for the *International Journal of Religious Education*.

"IN DEFENSE OF STORIES"

Hulda dedicated *Greatness Passing By* "to the Children of Bethel and to Cynthia," referring to Reinhold's congregation from 1916 to 1928, whom she had taught and led, and to her niece, daughter of H. Richard and Florence Mittendorf Niebuhr. Since her theory was always grounded in practice, it is not difficult to imagine that these stories had been written over many years for those children and told to them on many occasions when they were together.

That the Niebuhr home had been one devoted to learning, both academic and artistic, has been well documented. Reading both for pleasure and as a way to keep up with news, local, national, and international, was most likely a norm and expectation for all family members.

The stories Hulda wrote and collected in her book include three kinds of topics: stories with actual people, from unknown to well known, stories related to biblical characters or concepts, and general stories. Albert Schweitzer, Pierre and Marie Curie, Thomas Jefferson and Alexander Hamilton, and Johnny Appleseed provide illustrations of people concerned about making a positive contribution to the world in which they lived. Less well-known figures—immigrants to this country, scientists, a sheriff who worked toward prison reform, a woman medical missionary, a former slave who followed his dream of a musical career, a teacher of abandoned children—all serve to introduce readers to persons they might not meet in life. Such persons made a contribution to humankind, using the talents and gifts they possessed as ordinary human beings, sometimes in spite of the conditions in which they were raised.

The stories serve to inspire children to learn, to achieve, to aspire to their best, and most importantly to care for others. The more general stories—"Consequences," "Termites," "The Red Purse," and others—emphasize the importance of caring for others, of working together in community, of the consequence of one's actions, and of the ability of humans to grow and change in positive ways when they have the chance to experience positive nurturing environments that promote a sense of well-being, justice, and love.

Hulda demonstrated how each of the characters, no matter whether a little boy remembering to visit his grandfather or Marie Curie discovering radium, was an example of "greatness passing by." In understanding this, it is possible to perceive why Hulda chose to begin her book with a quote from John Drinkwater's *Abraham Lincoln, A Play*. "When the high heart we magnify, and the sure vision celebrate, and worship greatness passing by, ourselves are great."

The preface to her book includes two brief articles, "In Defense of Stories" and "The Telling of Stories." It is in these pages that Hulda articulated her method. She was concerned that storytelling was a discernible and teachable method in religious education, and she wanted it to be used correctly. The book without the preface would be a good collection of stories for younger youth to read. With the preface, the book becomes a resource for teachers and parents who would seek to understand the storytelling method and their role as tellers.

Hulda believed that stories appealed to the emotions and imaginations of the hearers and as such enabled the hearer to enter into new experiences, a new world. Stories had the power to present life and thus could be more powerful than actual life experiences.

> Actual, first-hand experiences can fail to have real experiential value. They may lack the perspective and informing power which a dramatic, interpretating [sic] story can give. It is possible for an individual to be so submerged in race hatred, for instance, that he cannot sense the meaning of race antagonisms as well as someone who has only tasted that experience through the condensed, spot-lighted insight which an interpreting great story has given and it may be that a story creates anew the universe after it has been annihilated in our minds by the recurrence of impressions blasted by reiteration.[48]

Hulda believed that there were four values of storytelling: (1) they make listeners and readers into creators—"The magic of the story's words causes the imagination of each hearer to work in an original, creative fashion even though the general pattern is indicated, for each imagination paints its screen with the pigments and shapes of its own interpretation, out of its own background of experience";[49] (2) stories engage the learner's imagination, feeling, and empathy with the characters; (3) stories provide a shortcut to experience; and (4) they represent a spread of values. The way that a story can "occasion fringe thoughts and fringe apprehensions is one of its assets."[50]

In "Telling Stories" Hulda contrasts the ineffectiveness of stories with "What Makes a Story."

> Sometimes a story is ineffective because it is a poor story, not worth the telling. Sometimes it is a good story in the wrong place. Often it is a good story in the right place, gone savorless because the teller is not prepared to tell it....Homiletic habits and lack of respect for children's intelligence get the best of the teller and he interrupts the action of the story to elucidate meanings.[51]

"What Makes a Story" is a poem written by Hulda for a class studying storytelling. She used verse, or "didactic doggerel" as she called it, to relate her instructions on how to tell a story. In the method of storytelling she was concerned with the choice of the story and the values it was communicating; the role of storytellers, how they presented the story to the hearer; the hearers and their stage of development; and the power of the story in its portrayal of "life condensed" and its appeal to the emotion and imagination of hearers. This method was one with which Hulda had great experience. She was concerned with teaching others the correct ways that stories should be used with children to enable positive learning experiences. An advertisement for the book notes that "its contents are in keeping with the high standard of modern educational methods."[52] Her book demonstrates how teaching young people requires attention to both content and process in order for creative learning to take place, a concern of twentieth century progressive educators.

Her book *Ventures in Dramatics* addressed a similar concern related to drama methods for children. Her purpose was to show through a collection of nineteen dramas how ten- through fifteen-year-old church school pupils were able to "lead a congregation in thought and worship."[53] Dedicated to Alberta Munkres and her coworkers at Madison Avenue Presbyterian Church, it too included an introduction with specific instructions regarding the developmental stage of children, the educational value and benefits of the method as it related to this particular age group, drama as a medium of expression, the danger of sincerity in dramatic productions, and the role of drama in religious education curriculum.

Hulda's study and work in Boston and her teaching experiences in the church provided her with a strong theoretical basis in understanding developmental growth of children. In the introductory section of the book, she was able to characterize clearly the developmental needs of children ages ten to fifteen and to identify in what ways dramatic activities would help to meet some of those needs.

She understood that younger adolescents wanted to achieve. They were concerned with gaining independence, self-respect, and the respect of others. She believed they were selective in their activities, choosing those that had a purpose and goal, ones that could make a difference. Hulda believed that this age group fell somewhere between an interest in spontaneous drama and finished productions. She found that drama, as a medium of expression, offered a challenge to the participants because it required expertise, the ability to pretend, the social aspects of working in a group, and a responsibility to the audience.

Just as she was most adamant and precise as to the process a storyteller used in telling a story, she was equally as precise in identifying the role of the leader in working with a group preparing a drama. The leader must be concerned with the kind of drama being presented, and the leader must be aware of how the group works together. "The reality and honesty of group activity are always endangered to whatever degree the leadership lacks insight to perceive problems objectively, or courage to deal with them fairly, or real regard for the welfare of all the pupils, or honest respect for their thinking and ability to guide it."[54] The needs of specific individuals must also be addressed, and the leader must examine her or his own role and the requirements expected of one who would work with youth in planning and participating in dramas in the church.

The plays in *Ventures and Dramatics* were probably all written and presented at Madison Avenue Presbyterian Church. They covered a variety of biblical stories, history, celebration of holidays, and life issues of younger adolescents. Each play includes a background section that describes how it came to be written and a manuscript of the dialog. Though youth leaders could have used the plays as written, their value was in demonstrating how teachers incorporate their understanding of the developmental needs of adolescents into their teaching using the method of drama. A review of this book described the plays as "drama projects...showing how each project developed through successive stages from its initial idea to presentation before an audience."[55]

The other writing that Hulda completed during her years at Madison Avenue Presbyterian Church were four articles that appeared in *The International Journal of Religious Education*. "Teaching the Bible to Junior Highs through Dramatization" appeared in the February 1941 issue. Though Hulda was illustrating how drama could enliven biblical study for younger youth, she was also concerned with how the Bible was used in teaching. "Their use of the Bible in class will be without zeal if the material is used only as proof text and if the stories are given only superficial study."[56] She closed the article with this comment about biblical study and this age group.

> They like to study the Bible stories just as history to see in them the interplay of personality, the swift moving drama, the setting in the history and the thought of the time. Sometimes there is something of a scholar's interest, as when pupils trace the development of worship, or compare different tellings of the same episode. They develop "sales resistance" against too wordy propagandizing, and some stories have become too hackneyed by superficial and sentimental repetitions to arouse interest. But when these junior-high boys and girls discover that in these stories they will find guidance for their own lives they respond eagerly to the opportunity to search for it.[57]

"Keep Them Near Thee" is an article describing a memorial service that younger youth planned for a Sunday worship service to remember relatives and friends serving in World War II. The initiative for this kind of service came from the group's concern for one of their members whose brother had been killed in battle. The article describes how the youth planned the service and includes the order of worship that they followed.

This article is significant in its description of the way that danger and death were dealt with by the leader and the group. The youth were obviously concerned about their friend whose brother had been killed. The teacher, probably Hulda, helped the group to discuss their concern and lead them into an activity that would provide an outlet for their emotions. Planning and leading this worship service also helped the youth to find a way to participate in helping to support those families whose children were serving in the war. An appropriate hymn was selected and sung at the service. "Since its interpretation on that Sunday the hymn is in the repertoire of the children's congregation and has been sung repeatedly in their Sunday morning worship as their prayer for the young men and women who are away from home in the service of their country."[58]

Hulda's writing during this period can be described as a synthesis of the theory and practice of religious education with children and youth. In each piece of writing, she demonstrated how teachers and leaders working with these age groups needed to understand what they were trying to communicate (content), to whom they were communicating (developmental stages of the young people), and how they were to communicate (teaching methods).

Hulda's articles and books were written with local church leaders and teachers in mind, hoping to inspire their creativity in teaching. In her articles Hulda illustrated through stories the ways that children learn and the kind of leadership needed from persons who would work with them.

The other freedom that Hulda enjoyed was teaching at New York University from 1938 to 1946. She had a contract with them to teach "Curriculum of the Church School," "Use of the Bible in the Lives of Boys and Girls," "Worship in the Church School," and "Supervision of Church School Teaching."[59]

An adjunct faculty relationship such as this one was made possible by Samuel L. Hamilton, chair of the Department of Religious Education in the School of Education of New York University from sometime during the 1930s until 1952. D. Campbell Wyckoff, a student in the program and later a faculty member, remembers Hamilton's policy.

One of his policies was to appoint as adjunct faculty outstanding practicing religious educators from the New York metropolitan area. They were chosen for excellence of performance in their fields of specialization and for their ability to interpret those fields in the classroom.[60]

Persons such as Hulda were expected to share incidents from their work, which the class could then use in discussion and critique. Wyckoff remembers that one focus for discussion in Hulda's classes were the weekly programs from the junior department from Madison Avenue Presbyterian Church.[61]

The freedoms Hulda had to write and to teach gave her the opportunity to reflect on her practice of religious education. These freedoms also required that she become proficient at interpreting her philosophy for others. Such work at this point in her life was essential in her continuing process of individuation and growth as an educator.

WOVEN THREADS

Four principles, which serve as the basis for Hulda Niebuhr's philosophy of religious education, emerge from her work at Madison Avenue Presbyterian Church. First, teaching and being were inseparable. Her beliefs about the infinite worth and value of all human beings and their ability to learn and grow defined the nature of her relationships with the people with whom she worked. Her work with teachers is a good example.

Teachers were trained and taught formally through courses of instruction. Informally, in numerous ways, volunteer teachers in the church school were valued and supported in the life of the church. Though there is no indication whether she was actually present, it is hard to imagine that Hulda Niebuhr's creativity and planning were not a part of luncheon meetings for church school teachers, monthly prayer sessions for teachers and officers of the church school, and meetings of parents and teachers of different departments of the church school. A newsletter article describes such a meeting of parents and teachers "to make plans for closer parent-teacher cooperation for next year. There will be on exhibit, the children's work, pamphlets and books for use in family worship and suggestions for home worship centers."[62]

Two additional resources for teachers provided by the church were a teachers' reference library and a *Teacher's Bulletin*, which was edited by Hulda. In 1938, a special issue focused on the issue of peace and war. "Whatever the needs of any class, all Christian teachers will need to be thinking about the problem of peace and war on their own account, and many of us are baffled."[63] Hulda went on to make reference to an earlier issue of the journal, *Social Action*, which had been placed in the teachers' library. She encouraged teachers to read it for suggestions to deal with the realities of the day.

Hulda's second principle emphasized learning that was experiential, reflective, and transformative and that assumed responsibility on the part of the learner. An article which Hulda wrote, "Candy and the Kingdom, How One Group Found an Interesting Pathway to Heroes of Social Welfare," described her use of a praxis model of religious education beginning with the experience of the learners to lead a group of youth in discovering areas of social responsibility in their own backyard. A discussion of candy bars led to questions about production and work standards: wages, regulated hours, and safety on the job. After learning about laws for the protection of the factory workers, the youth developed a list of those candy factories whose working conditions conformed to legal guidelines. Their research then focused on learning about social welfare workers, including Jane Adams, Frances Perkins, Lord Shaftesbury, and William Lloyd Garrison. Their discoveries were shared in a Sunday service of worship for their age group.

In the beginning of the article, Hulda had made the observation that

our pupils really live in a bigger world than the school, a bigger world even than comprises the school and the home and the church. Juniors and intermediates at least are old enough to live in a bigger world.... The Parable of the Good Samaritan may have been learned letter perfect, or it may have been dramatized in a manner that evidences a fine interplay of pupil activity and increase of social aptitude, without having anything happen to make pupils more sensitive and apt in their responsibilities in relation to the race problem in their own community. A school may have a well developed system of budget administration by the pupils without making them conscious of any wider ethical, and may we not say religious, implications of some of their own economic experiences.[64]

Hulda reported that at the close of the service of worship when the juniors presented their findings, and after she reminded them about the list and encouraged them to boycott candy from nonapproved factories, the youth said: "Please let us not take out our religion only in praying to be good. We are not yet old enough to help make laws by voting. Let us do something about this matter that we know we can do."[65]

Hulda's third principle was that the church was a faithful Christian community, a place where people were both nurtured and challenged in their faith. For Hulda, the church was a place of learning that equipped people with knowledge of biblical content as well as analytical and critical thinking abilities to apply that knowledge in their lives in the world. Central to her understanding of the church was its inclusive and ecumenical nature. The church was a place where all ages and races could feel welcome and included. She was most concerned that children be involved in all aspects of the church's life, work and ministry.

The ecumenical vision that had been a part of Hulda's experience growing up in the Evangelical church was also an important part of her ministry at Madison Avenue Presbyterian Church. Consistent with the Christian hope and vision of her first community of faith, Madison Avenue Church offered Hulda a place in which she could work to expand people's understanding of the ecumenical and multicultural nature and mission of the church in the world.

Finally, the purpose of Christian education for Hulda Niebuhr was to enable the growth in Christian faith of persons so that they could live their lives in response to the biblical story. In an article she wrote after she had joined the faculty at McCormick Theological Seminary, she expressed it this way:

Christian education is the believing community at work helping people listen and look in order that by God's grace they may hear and see and so be helped to know the hope to which they are called by God in Jesus Christ.[66]

The task involved the creative presentation of "the story of salvation so that it may become a part of each individual's own history, absorbed into the context of his own particular life, be he young or older, rich or poor, from East or West."[67] Obvious in these statements are concerns for who the learners are, what they bring to the teaching-learning process, communication of the biblical story, and the integration of the biblical story into personal life individually as Christians and corporately in a community of faith. Perhaps Hulda's greatest creative contribution was awakening and encouraging that ability in other people as they sought to find ways to express their faith in God.

Hulda Niebuhr took advantage of the great freedom she was given at Madison Avenue Presbyterian Church to strengthen their day-to-day program of religious education with children, youth, and adults. Hulda and the people of the church came together and their faith commitments were strengthened as a result of the encounter.

Hulda believed that grounding in the Christian faith "is accomplished more successfully when children actually participate in the fellowship, concerns, and programs of the church, and when they are confronted in actual experience with such interpretative factors as the Bible, and Christian history and tradition."[68] Equally important for her was the conviction that a church's program of Christian education can "be effective only when the entire church accepts responsibility for it and is concerned about extending its influence in the community, when all members care deeply about teaching religion through the home, and the church, and about enlisting children and youth."[69]

The effectiveness of her leadership within Madison Avenue Presbyterian Church is clearly stated in the article that announced her resignation from the church staff.

> Largely as a result of her intelligence and indefatigability, coupled with inflexible honesty in word and action, her creativeness, her staunch social-mindedness, her appreciation of the meaning and value of true worship, her Biblically-based philosophy of Christian Education, her understanding of life and deftness in helping people in their religious growth, her intuitive sense of spiritual values, her inspiring cooperation and her Christian zeal, our Church School has come to be known as an effective part of the life of our parish.[70]

Hulda's work at the church helped her to discover the depth, richness, and variety of threads that wove together religious educational theory and practice.

Hulda teaching at McCormick Theological Seminary, Chicago

4

Beyond Notebooks (1946–1959)

PHOTOGRAPHS OF HULDA NIEBUHR that help to capture her during this period of her life always show her with other people. One picture shows her standing in front of her home with one of her students, who also served as a teaching assistant. Another shows Hulda seated on the ground with students involved in discussion at a retreat setting.

She is pictured more formally seated next to her mother, her hands folded in her lap. This picture, along with one that shows mother and daughter in academic robes, was taken on the occasion of Lydia Niebuhr receiving an honorary degree from Lindenwood College and Hulda presenting the Founder's Day address. For Hulda, the years at McCormick were ones of intense involvement in her teaching, with her students, and with the McCormick community.

The Niebuhr home at 850 Chalmers Place, a row house on the inside circle of the McCormick Theological Seminary campus on the north side of Chicago, was a place of activity and hospitality. No one was ever turned away from the Niebuhr home. Especially welcome were children of faculty, administrators, and students, as well as children from the neighborhood. The spouse of a McCormick student remembered Hulda's hospitality in this way:

> We were privileged to have two children with us at McCormick just after World War II when veterans were attending Seminary. So we appreciated her interest in not only faculty children but students' children as well. She invited me to attend her child psychology class and bring my two children to be observed. I did. Ready for us was a blanket on the floor and toys for the children. She carried on her class with little notice from the occupied and "at ease" children and mother.[1]

What had been primarily an adult community changed drastically as younger faculty members and students arrived with their children or ready to start their families. Hulda and Lydia's interest, natural abilities, and love for children provided the spark that transformed the nature of community life on the seminary campus.

During the early spring of 1945, correspondence began between the president of McCormick Theological Seminary in Chicago and Hulda Niebuhr. President Harry Cotton was seeking an instructor in children's work for the Presbyterian College of Christian Education, a small, two-year graduate school supported by the Presbyterian church with a faculty of five. Located across the street from each other, the schools maintained a cooperative relationship.

In a letter of response to President Cotton's first letter, Hulda showed an interest in pursuing a conversation, though she felt "that the limitation of 'children's work' you speak of is interesting to me, I feel it a limitation as I like a wider range and have given much time to adolescents and youth."[2] The correspondence during this period of negotiations between Hulda and McCormick reveals a woman certain of herself as a professional, articulate about her interests in teaching, and assertive about her rights as a single, professional woman.

At this point in her career, Hulda had vast experience both as an educator working with local congregations and as a professor in two graduate schools. She had recognition in her professional field as author, teacher, and practitioner. The offer to join the faculty of the Presbyterian College represented another step on her journey to name her theory of religious education.

> I have come to a tested philosophy of religious education that I am in the process of writing down, have developed our own curriculum here

[Madison Avenue Presbyterian Church], and I have thoroughly enjoyed the teaching I have done in the latter years in New York
University for now I feel I am not talking out of notebooks, but I have
hammered out a position that I feel is mine, out of years of experience
with many people.[3]

Hulda brought to the College of Christian Education and to McCormick
Theological Seminary the experience and wisdom of a professional educator who understood both the academic and professional requirements for
those preparing for the profession of religious educator or minister.

This next step in her journey represented a venture into areas that were
unknown. Again she would make a move to another educational institution.
She probably wondered what direction her professional career was headed
during these last years before retirement. Having served as an assistant
professor in 1925 at Boston University and as a lecturer at New York
University from 1932 to 1946, she was now, at age fifty-six, being offered
a position as instructor.

Uprooting herself and leaving family and friends could not have been
easy for her or her mother, who was seventy-four. It was probably assumed
by Hulda's brothers that Lydia Niebuhr would continue to live with Hulda
and make the move to Chicago. Hulda must have considered how her mother
would react to leaving her church, her son Reinhold and his family, and to
making a new home on the seminary campus. Hulda also must have thought
about her age and health as well as her mother's.

By this point in her life, Hulda knew her physical limitations and her
tendency toward exhaustion from overcommitment to her work. In moving
her mother with her, she also realized they would be at a distance from her
brothers. H. Richard was in New Haven with his family, teaching at Yale.
Reinhold and his family remained in New York, where he was teaching at
Union Theological Seminary. Walter was living with his family in New
York when he died of a heart attack in 1946. The move to Chicago meant
that for the first time in her life, Hulda would have total responsibility for
making a home for herself and her mother.

The move also represented starting over, putting down new roots at a time
in life when her friends were enjoying longtime friends and considering
their future years of retirement. In contrast, Hulda faced challenge and
transition in a new career as professor in a denominational seminary and life
with a new community on the seminary campus. The future, rather than
being predictable and known, was open and expectant with possibilities for
continued individuation and self-development.

CONSIDERING THE MOVE

In a letter written to the president of McCormick two months before she moved to Chicago, Hulda described the members of the curriculum class she was teaching at New York University:

> a missionary from Latvia, one from Indo-China, the promotion secretary of the Church of the Brethren, a major in the Salvation Army who is supervising the religious education of the Army in eleven states, and the Salvation Army head of the educational work in New York City,...a Lutheran and a Methodist deaconess, the supervisor of the weekday religious education in Salem, Oregon, herself a Methodist lay preacher,...a 40-year-old policeman,...an elderly industrialist widow who is superintendent of a Junior Department; a young Norwegian who broadcast religious messages to Norway under the OWI during the war, a teacher in the Missionary Alliance Training School.[4]

Hulda speculated that there would "be a different kind of fun in teaching a homogeneous group of young Presbyterians."[5] Such musings caused her to consider the variety of backgrounds in the students in her class at New York University. "Do you suppose there could be a possibility of a denominational school serving that kind of group?"[6]

Hulda must have wondered what it would be like to be associated with a denominational seminary after having been removed from that kind of teaching for fifteen years. Perhaps she also was considering what difference the "homogeneous group of young Presbyterians" would mean in terms of her own teaching. Obviously she had felt challenged by the variety of experience and theological perspective of students in her classes at New York University. Hulda must have been thinking about where she would find this kind of variety and challenge in a Presbyterian seminary.

Once again Hulda had placed herself in the position of starting over. She was obviously prepared for and committed to taking another step on the journey, one that would complete her career and her life and thus serve to name her theory of religious education.

McCormick Theological Seminary and the Presbyterian College of Christian Education were graduate schools on their own journey of seeking students, faculty, and financial resources. The college, which offered a master of arts in Christian education, had an expected enrollment of thirty for the school year 1945–46 and enjoyed a close working relationship with the seminary. Students enrolled in one institution were free to take classes at the other.

The way had been paved for this cooperation by the action of the college in 1942, when they voted to accept only students with a college degree. Most students were women preparing themselves for careers as educators in the church. One hundred thirty-seven men were enrolled in the seminary in 1945. McCormick Theological Seminary was about to embark on a campaign to raise $1 million, and conversations had already been initiated regarding a merger of the two schools.

Harry Cotton, president of McCormick, suggested in a letter to Hulda the reality of the college. "It has struggled along here for more than thirty years with a small student body and a faculty made up of people who were brought in from the outside for special courses. It is now beginning to get on its feet. This year we have a faculty of five."[7]

It is obvious from the correspondence between Cotton and Hulda that the position they were seeking to fill changed during the discussion. The college needed an instructor in children's work. The annual report of the Presbyterian College of Christian Education for 1944 described a hopeful future for the school.

The Boards of Christian Education, National Missions, and Foreign Missions have indicated support that is making it possible for us to recruit a faculty that will command the respect of the Church. Already, the Board of Directors of the College has approved a salary scale for the College identical with that of the seminary. It is expected that we shall have a full-time faculty composed of a Dean, Professor of Education, Professor of Bible, Professor of Social Work, Professor of Missions and Instructor in Children's Work by the opening of the Fall Term. We are searching for recognized leaders in these fields.[8]

Considering Hulda's age, work in the church, published works, and academic record with two institutions, it seems strange that the college would open their conversation with her by offering a position at the lowest rank, instructor. The other positions mentioned in the annual report were all filled by males. From reading the annual report, it is possible to conclude that the leaders of the college were concerned that their students receive instruction that would focus both on theory and practice. Perhaps in their hope to find a "recognized leader in the field" of children's work, they had not considered that a woman with Hulda's credentials would exist.

The position that was eventually offered to Hulda was associate professor of religious education. During the negotiations, another member of the college faculty resigned. The president of the seminary, who also served as president of the college, indicated that the position would not be filled until after Hulda had arrived. He promised that she would be included in the conversations with the other professor of Christian education, James S. Armentrout. Hulda was eventually hired as associate professor at an annual salary of $3,200, including housing, pension, and moving expenses.

After interviews and correspondence lasting over a one-year period, Harry Cotton had become convinced of Hulda's ability as a teacher and wanted nothing to serve as an obstacle to her appointment to the faculty. The correspondence reveals Hulda's five concerns: (1) when she was to begin her teaching; (2) where she was to live; (3) what she was to teach; (4) her commitment to research and scholarship; and (5) her vision for her teaching. In each case her assertive response to Cotton's proposals enabled her to establish the strength of her voice and the certainty of her conviction when dealing with the administration of the Presbyterian College of Christian Education.

Early in the negotiations, Hulda expressed a desire to begin her teaching during the winter quarter of the school year 1945–46, which began on February 26, 1946. Her resignation at Madison Avenue Presbyterian Church was accepted and became effective on September 1, 1945. During the fall of 1945 she was scheduled to teach a curriculum course at New York University and believed that she must honor this commitment. In a letter to Cotton she wrote:

> For some time I have had in mind that I wanted to express to you my gratitude for your understanding my desire for a sabbatical semester before coming to Chicago. Without you the pressure for immediate help in the school there would have carried. I am having a most profitable interim, enjoying life on the three months salary the church gave me as a parting gift, studying and writing, teaching a very exciting class at the university.[9]

In an earlier letter to Cotton she had indicated that New York University had "wanted me to give them more time but for a number of years I have taught a course at a time, in the Department of Religious Education, all that I could do in addition to my work at the church here."[10]

During the sabbatical that she took before going to McCormick, Hulda was a student at Teacher's College, Columbia University, where she had pursued doctoral studies fifteen years earlier. Her transcript shows that she took three courses during the first quarter of 1945–46. Two were in the area of curriculum and teaching. "Educational Programs for Children" examined the relationship between the life of the school, the home, and other "educational agencies of the community; utilization of the resources of science, art, music, language, and other fields for the development of children."[11] "The Arts in Childhood Education" course was "designed to give students an opportunity for art experiences and the development of art skills through direct experiences in various media."[12] The third course she took was in the speech department, "Choral Speaking."

These courses represented areas of special interest and focus in her teaching. Her enrollment in these classes gives evidence that she perceived this sabbatical as a time to nurture her professional needs. It was the first time since her days as a graduate student after moving to New York in 1928 that Hulda had given herself that kind of opportunity. The extra income from Madison Avenue Presbyterian Church and the time given her by McCormick Seminary made this sabbatical possible.

Hulda used this time to prepare herself mentally and physically for leaving New York. Relationships and feeling a part of community were important to her. "The sorrows and pleasures, of saying goodbye here have begun. I must include pleasures. Next Sunday, for instance, the Sunday School will dramatize characters from 'Greatness Passing By.'"[13]

The visit to McCormick in April 1945 and her lengthy correspondence with President Harry Cotton helped her accommodate successfully to the "in between life" of saying goodbyes and hellos. She commented in a letter during the summer of 1945 that she "felt established as a member of your academic family even while leaving the church family here."[14] While keeping the communications open and moving, Hulda was successful in delaying her move to Chicago until the time when she was ready. It was important to her to honor her teaching commitment at New York University as well as to have time for her own study, relaxation, and preparation for this next step in her journey.

A second concern that consumed much time, thought, and negotiation before her arrival was focused on her living accommodations. The move to the Presbyterian College of Christian Education was perceived differently by Hulda than by Armentrout, dean of the college, who assumed that Hulda would be willing to live in the dorm with women students since there was no faculty housing available at the time. Besides administration, dining, dormitories, library, and classrooms, the seminary also owned four-story row houses that served as residences for faculty members.

From the beginning of the correspondence about the move, the issue of Hulda's mother was a priority. Early in the negotiations it was decided that since a faculty apartment on the campus was not immediately available, Lydia Niebuhr would wait until the summer to move. Hulda, frustrated by the unrealistic expectations of Armentrout, finally articulated to the president that "we are really not a family of only two" and that plans to house her in a dorm was not acceptable.

> It makes me very happy indeed to have a roomy house to think about as a future home. Last spring when I returned from Chicago I promised several of the young people at our church, toward whom I have been acting sort of "in loco parentis," that they might have a home with me while getting an education.... As age advances upon my mother it will be necessary [to] find a full time housekeeper to stay with us. Also, there is my mother's sister, a retired deaconess who has always been very close to our family.... My brothers and my nieces and nephews will enjoy staying with us in their various goings and comings if we have a guest room at disposal.[15]

The possibility of moving into a faculty row house on Chalmers Square became a reality but only after a year of negotiation. At issue for Armentrout was the expense and availability of housing off campus when housing in a dorm was available. At issue for Hulda was her privacy, her health, room for her family, and a place to allow separation of her work and her home. Communication about this issue, which had begun with Armentrout, was redirected to President Cotton as Hulda successfully attempted to assert her own needs for independence. President Harry Cotton took the role of mediator between the college and Hulda and became a strong advocate for Hulda's position.

It is obvious that Hulda was concerned both about her needs and those of the institution. A double room in the school dormitory had been offered to her and she accepted it at first since she "felt that it was no time to say anything about liking privacy and finding life in such a group a drain upon energy."[16] She knew that other women faculty "were content with dormitory rooms and that three months are not an eternity.... Harmony on the campus would be a first consideration."[17]

Two days after writing the letter accepting dormitory accommodations, she followed with another one that more clearly stated her feelings and desires about housing. Revealed in this exchange of letters is a woman concerned both with her needs and how her statement of those needs would be perceived by the institution. Acknowledging her personal preference for housing and the reasons to support it also meant that this private person had to risk revealing something about herself both to herself and to the president and had to trust a relative stranger with such confidential and personal information.

I shall have a heavier program than first anticipated. With the community training school there will be ten hours of teaching the first five weeks and then eight. All the work will be new for I have not taught the two college courses before (not that I have not taught much of the content in some way or other) and a community class is always different because you get such a wide range of needs. In a last semester of the year and with a new teacher there also will be more personal interviews than usual. I think it would be a full program for any physique and temperament but I always have to hoard my energy because I use so much when I am with people. For some reason I don't like to acknowledge that fact, (the people at Madison don't know how much time I spent resting when I was not on deck) but I might as well tell it.[18]

In a letter dated December 18, 1945, she referred to the idea of living in the dorm as a handicap. "What had been a dormant small disquiet awoke to a feeling that I had—written off [as a] handicap which may not be inevitable."[19] In a response to her letter, Cotton assured her of his commitment.

In your last letter you wrote very well about writing of any handicap that proves inevitable. That's alright [sic] for inevitable handicap, but why go out of the way to [find] one? What I am saying is this—I think in your second letter you spoke your own real purpose and desire, and I for one certainly agree with it. I think you need a quiet place to withdraw and be by yourself. That is certainly not a selfish desire, and I think the best interests of the college would be served if you did so.[20]

The issue was finally settled satisfactorily for both sides, and Hulda was able to write at the beginning of the new year, "I saw dormitory life as an unnecessary handicap, and I am ever so glad you rule it to be unnecessary. The 'fly in the ointment' is gone."[21]

A room at the Webster Hotel was reserved for Hulda in order to give her time to find other temporary housing. The options offered to Hulda were a room in a house near to the campus or a semiprivate room in the dormitory on the campus. Considering her strong preference for housing, it is more likely that Hulda stayed in the house off campus or in the hotel.

Beyond negotiations regarding housing, Hulda had indicated, from the beginning of the conversations about teaching, that she found the area of concentration in children's work to be too confining. In her correspondence with Armentrout, she made as little progress regarding teaching as she had on the issue of housing.

Dr. Armentrout and I are in communication about courses. At the risk of seeming too insistent, I keep expressing the hope that before very long I shall teach in the field that has engrossed most of my attention these last years. Junior High and High, particularly the former. The churches lose that age youngsters, teachers and ministers say they do not know what to do with them. Leadership in that field is urgently needed. It feels wasteful to me to put my experience there into cold storage and be altogether a little children's worker. I won't belabor the point, just see it is not lost.[22]

Hulda had realized that President Cotton's help was needed as a mediator between herself and the college on yet another issue. Again he took her side.

I quite agree with you that you should not confine yourself to the methods of little children. I think you would do very well to insist with Dr. Armentrout that next year you will give one course on young people's work. I know that many of the seminary students would want to take that course under you. After all you will have ample freedom to name your own electives—courses which you feel best qualified to give.[23]

Hulda also gave evidence of the priority of research and scholarship in her field. By 1945, it had been ten years since her second book had been published. In her first letter to President Cotton she suggested that she had "come to a tested philosophy of religious education that I am in the process of writing down."[24] In her "Professional and Academic Record" that she compiled for McCormick, she indicated that she was working on two manuscripts. One was on worship in the church school and the other was on her philosophy of Christian education, "which latter is to have a much less imposing title than that since the writer is not a philosopher—but it still will be a philosophy stated."[25] In a later letter she said that "my two books can't possibly be finished before I come, but the spade work will be done and a summer or two will finish them."[26]

Like many other new faculty members joining an academic community, Hulda probably found herself overwhelmed with the responsibilities of planning and teaching new courses, meeting new students and colleagues, and managing the demands of teaching and speaking engagements with the need for personal time. Arriving as the only woman on a faculty with a majority of women students, she probably also experienced demands on her time as a professional woman with experience in a career for which her students were preparing. Hulda's heavy schedule undoubtedly left little time and energy for writing, for her published writing after arriving in

Chicago was limited to journals and articles for the McCormick alumni publication, *McCormick Speaking.*

During her negotiations for the McCormick position, Hulda clearly articulated her convictions and expectations regarding the purpose of religious education in the local congregation. She had no doubts about her vision for teaching educators and ministers preparing themselves for work with congregations. For Hulda, more important than courses in Christian education was an attitude in the seminary that helped make seminarians "alive to their inevitable responsibility in relation to Christian nurture in their parishes and communities."[27] She was concerned with what must have been a prevailing attitude that responsibilities in Christian education could be passed on to a person hired for that job. If a minister did not have an educator with whom to work or if the minister "is too handicapped to do anything about it,…the work of the evangelization of youth won't go forward very fast."[28]

Hulda continued her comments to President Cotton, saying that she had learned a lot by watching the young men from Union Seminary who had worked with the staff at Madison Avenue Presbyterian Church and was convinced how "much can be done in churches and communities where a minister accepts responsibility—and also has some practical ideas and skills."[29] She was concerned about equipping pastors with both attitudes toward Christian education and skills that would enable them to assume their responsibilities in Christian nurture. She was also interested in the ecumenical possibilities for the study of religious education at McCormick.

I am quite excited about the interest some Methodists showed in our school in Chicago. Every where people are saying what they said: that the field of religious education needs centers for leadership training, that any work so strategic must have more attention from the church. These leaders on Saturday [missionaries from a variety of denominations] said that denominational differences made no difference "where training is given in a way that is thoroughly Christian and effective." They would like to bring up a group of leaders, they said, with *experience* in working with other denominations constructively.[30]

The journey that finally brought Hulda to McCormick involved skills of diplomacy, negotiation, and assertiveness. She was able to grasp quickly the politics of the situation and to figure out that she had an advocate in the president to help meet her expectations while keeping the administration of the college appraised of his actions.

It is equally clear that Hulda was taking a step into a situation about which she was not naive. When she was asked to send a bibliography for her classes, she responded with a detailed explanation of the kinds of books she would need and asked about a book budget available to her. In this letter to President Cotton she went on to say, "If I ought to send this list to Dean Armentrout, do not hesitate in the least to say so. I don't know yet how to feel my way in matters that straddle Seminary and College. . . . I am sure you both [Cotton and Armentrout] will let me use your patience while I learn my way."[31]

It is obvious that she was sensitive to political issues, lines of authority, and the need to make a smooth entry into a new institution. Hulda did not hesitate to tackle issues important to her personal being, to her teaching, and to her relationship with the administration. It must have been clear to the administration of the seminary and the college that the woman they had hired was an articulate, competent, and assertive professional.

A PHILOSOPHY OF TEACHING

Hulda served on the faculty of the Presbyterian College of Christian Education from February 1946 until its merger with McCormick Theological Seminary in 1949. With her colleagues from the college, Professors James Armentrout and Vartan Melconian and Associate Professor John Mixon, she became a regular member of the McCormick faculty teaching in the Division of Christian Education and Social Work within the seminary. Hulda was made a full professor in 1952 and held that appointment until her death on April 17, 1959, the spring in which she was to retire from teaching.

Hulda's writing during these years provides insight into what she believed was essential to prepare ministers and educators for educational ministry. Three concepts were predominant in her writing and teaching and served as foundations for her philosophy.

The first of these principles, intentional religious nurture, was a quality that Hulda inherited directly from her membership in the Niebuhr family. One of her former students said that "she came with undisputed credentials. Everyone knew Reinhold Niebuhr. Most knew Richard Niebuhr. I remember hearing in a lunch line that she was 'of the family.' The family was something to be 'of.'"[32]

Lydia and Gustav were parents who shared their natural talents and interests so that their children both learned and experienced the realities of the Christian faith. Ronald Stone observed that the Niebuhr home provided a "secure setting which gave deep religious foundation to all the children. It also imbued them with a fervor for the values of freedom and equality and a high priority to the values of the academic life."[33]

Intentional religious nurture was inherent in Hulda's teaching. Two pieces of her writing illustrate how she interpreted the difference between Christianity as a cultural norm and Christianity as response and commitment, which is bequeathed to us by our "spiritual progenitors." Hulda stated this explicitly in the Founder's Day address that she gave at Lindenwood College on October 17, 1953. It is appropriate that the topic of her speech, "Spiritual Progenitors," was given at the time Lydia H. Niebuhr was awarded an honorary doctorate of humanities from the college.

Hulda's article in *The Pulpit*, "Spiritual Progenitors," represents most of that Founder's Day address. A portion of the address is also included in the article "Are We Raising Nominal Christians?" which she wrote for *McCormick Speaking*. "Spiritual Progenitors" addresses the issue of how we pass on our faith to others. "Do we really stand in that line of parents, pastors, teachers, neighbors, citizens whose influence was of such order that they may be thought of as spiritual progenitors, ancestors, forebears, people whose faith kindled the faith of others?"[34]

Hulda believed that the role of spiritual progenitor called for helping others "into that higher model of living which is eternal life" and as such is not a role that is a matter of age.[35] Spiritual progenitors were contrasted with nominal Christians who understood Christianity as an easy religion that believed in an understanding God. According to Hulda, complacent, nominal, conventional Christians had the right form but lacked the spirit. The problem, as she saw it, was that nominal Christians lived in conformity to the world.

> To say that we are living in a day when we are especially tempted to live conventionally respectable lives, says in effect that we are living in a day of conformity. The rewards seem to go, in many communities, to the teacher, the minister, the politician, the voter, commentator, playwright, who takes no risks in moving counter to prevalent trends.[36]

To illustrate her concern about form and spirit, Hulda used the analogy of music: "It is much easier to play the notes of a composer's score than to play in such a manner that his spirit and feeling are conveyed."[37] She claimed that nominal Christians responded complacently to the demands of God and as such were incapable of being spiritual progenitors for anyone. Humility and love were two attributes that Hulda noted as essential to helping a Christian feel the spirit of the faith. She tied together private and public faith in the concept of life in God and life under God that she believed as "two aspects of the same reality. The obedience God asks is seldom something separate from our relations to others."[38]

In her article "Are We Raising Nominal Christians?" Hulda emphasized the idea of the church as Christian community, where people of all ages could experience the duality of life that produces a heritage of spiritual progenitors. In the article she quoted from the definition of "witness" in "The Ecumenical Survey" prepared for the Commission on Evangelism for the World Council Meeting of 1954. "The life witness of the entire community encompasses and qualifies every spoken word. The proclamation is always situated in a total life context."[39] Hulda believed that it was only in such a context as a living and witnessing community that it was possible for form to be alive.

Gustav Niebuhr spoke of the necessity of each church committing itself to claiming a new vision of its calling by God to the world. Hulda was colleague both with her father in his mission work and with her mother in the many volunteer assignments she accepted in the pastorates of Hulda's father and brother Reinhold. Both of Hulda's parents demonstrated the obedience to God of which she is speaking. Thus, as spiritual progenitors for their children, Gustav and Lydia provided the kind of Christian home where both the form and the spirit of the faith were encouraged to develop and mature.

One way of understanding Hulda's own development and individuation in her work is to discover in what way she was a "spiritual progenitor" for others. A former student commented on a statement that Hulda made in class. "Learning process was something to the effect that what curriculum is used doesn't matter as much as who the teacher is. It is the personal life and faith, the integrity and Christian expression of the teacher which determines ultimately what happens in the classroom."[40]

Evidently what Hulda believed about spiritual progenitors was demonstrated in the kind of teacher she modeled for her students.

There was an atmosphere in the class that education was growth and must be related to experience (doing). There was a high regard for the importance of each member of the class—often our projects would be evaluated by our peers. I do not recall anyone ever being humiliated in class. Also, we were encouraged to get out of the class what we put into it—nothing came from just being there. Consequently, we all learned from our outside reading, from doing our projects, and from each other. Creativity was encouraged, imagination was stimulated.[41]

Many students have commented on the experience of being in the Niebuhr home on the McCormick campus. Students were often invited over for refreshments and informal conversation with Hulda and her mother. Invitations to their home, a custom which Hulda shared with Reinhold and H. Richard, were described by Georgie Frame Madison, a student of Hulda's who upon graduation was employed by McCormick as a fieldwork supervisor, assisting Hulda's students in the Division of Christian Education.

As a student, I with others was often invited to the house for little meetings or evenings of fellowship.... I well remember the evening we students were invited over to meet her son. I can't say now whether it was Reinhold or Richard, but I know that we all sat on the living room floor, literally at his feet and were so impressed as we listened. In these informal meetings at the house, we students talked with Hulda about her interest in Chicago politics (which really didn't concern us very much, though she thought they should), her great interest in Eleanor Roosevelt and the work of the fledgling U.N. Committee on Human Rights, which at the time was meeting in San Francisco. And at those little gatherings we'd hear about our McCormick/Chalmers Place neighborhood beyond the classroom, especially about the faculty children and their doings, for both Mrs. and Miss Niebuhr were greatly endeared to the Chalmers Place children. There were always several sitting on their doorstep.[42]

Two other comments from students illustrate the kind of spiritual progenitor Hulda was in the classroom. One has said that she always seemed to be in a hurry. "She was too darn busy to worry about making a mark."[43] Another student said that she "understood making a mark in a different way—to produce effective, creative teachers. Her mark was to be made in the classroom, otherwise she was inconsistent in her own assumptions."[44] The mark Hulda Niebuhr made theologically is visible not in volumes of writing but in the form and spirit of a few selected pieces and in her life as a teacher as it has been embodied in her students. "My keenest remembrance is that I realized much growth in that class—personal growth, growth in ability, interpersonal growth (social), and an increasing growth in admiration for a wonderful person and teacher."[45]

A second concept that captures an important theme in Hulda's teaching and writing focuses on her understanding of developmental theory, teaching/learning activities appropriate for children and youth, and classroom methods most useful in preparing adults to work with young people.

Her study and research as well as her years of practical experience working with young people provided Hulda with a philosophy of a congregational approach to ministry with children and youth. What was essential was a church's understanding that "it must minister to all its constituency."[46] In a survey she conducted with fifty seminary alumni who had experience working in the church, she received these responses:

"I make it a point to know all my children and call them by name,"... "Know children as persons," "Treat them as individual personalities"—these are recurring refrains, along with "Know how children think," "Visit public schools" to learn what engages them during school hours and how they are taught there.[47]

She showed this concern in her work with her students. "It was her showing how the Arts could be incorporated into teaching that helped me see where my music avocation was to be incorporated into my Christian Education career. She taught us arts, crafts, and drama which helped us (by experience) to see where and how to use them with the various age levels."[48] Hulda was convinced that churches should take seriously the mandate to "Feed my lambs" and by doing so could learn "to be the church in relation to all its members."[49]

One very public way that congregations could demonstrate the intentionality and integrity of their ministry with children was in the use of children's sermons during worship. Hulda's definition of the junior sermon illustrates the tension she observed between using abstract object lessons and more age appropriate methods.

Junior Sermon: From three to five minutes in length and designed to meet the needs of boys and girls who attend Sunday morning worship....Normal ages are approximately from six to twelve....While the literature of the subject is abundant, any that gives systematic guidance is scanty. So called "object-lessons" and parable sermons, prevalent in the past are being superseded. In a day with more general understanding of child psychology and educational principles, leaders prefer other types, notably stories, including those from the Bible. Through stories boys and girls identify themselves with people whose experience clarifies, heightens, or interprets their own. They also make their own applications, an opportunity denied them in sermons given to moralization.[50]

Hulda contrasted the analogical children's sermon, "a misdirected effort because it is not understood by children," with the telling of a good biblical story.[51]

We bemoan the fact that our church members do not know the Bible, while at the same time we waste opportunities to make it available to them. Children (not to mention adults) like to hear good stories told and retold. The Bible teems with dramatic material that can be presented to them directly, in the story form.[52]

Hulda believed that appropriate children's sermons could open the door to learning just as abstract object lessons could do "nothing to clarify their [the children's] own problems or to bring inspiration beyond the wish to please a minister whom they like."[53]

An earlier article illustrated Hulda's knowledge of and experience with adolescents and the difficulty of knowing when to say yes and when to say no. In "Yes and No" she succinctly described the difficulty of transition young people face during adolescence and the kind of leadership needed to help them move successfully through this stage of development. One section of the article makes clear her thesis.

> Though the junior high is unsure of his abilities, he is very conscious of them. There is nothing he normally wants or needs more than to use them as his own initiative suggests.... If his educators have been wise, he has had more and more opportunity since infancy to exercise his capacity for independent action. The more confidence and self-assurance he has gained through this kind of experience during childhood, the less strained will be his demand now for independence.... The more poise he has learned from the Christian fellowship in church and home, the more stable he will be, and the less he will fear frustration or nurse hurts when they come. If his development is wholesome, he will now wish to "untie the apron strings" and stand on his feet.[54]

She concludes the article with these final words of advice for those who live or work with adolescents.

> "No" is bad when we say it because, consciously or unconsciously, we need the child's dependence as a prop for our own ego.... "Yes" is bad when we say it for fear of losing our standing with our pupils.... Self-love in a parent or a teacher can keep him from seeing clearly the need of young persons in his charge. When we love them truly, we need have no fear of losing our authority. We use it calmly when we must—and then find that we have not lost it, because they trust us.[55]

This concern for the relationship between developmental theory and its application in working with children and adolescents in the church was also evident in the kinds of teaching methods Hulda used in her classes.

Though course descriptions in the seminary catalogs do not indicate which professors taught specific courses, it is probably safe to assume that

Hulda taught the Curriculum of Christian Education, Curriculum Writing and Religious Journalism, Christian Education of Children, Growth and Development of the Child, and Christian Education of Adolescents. The course in growth and development was added to the curriculum in 1947 and the course in curriculum writing and journalism in 1955. The other three courses had been listed in the catalog since 1945.

Three methods used by Hulda illustrate ways that she encouraged her students to use their creativity in their teaching in order to "know children as persons." Dramatic play as a way of "trying on life" was one favorite method. She taught her students how to enable children and youth to present dramas as well as how to write them. She believed that dramatization of biblical material could "further the objects of Bible study."[56] Noting this emphasis in the teaching of young people, one of her students commented on another aspect of Hulda's teaching and learning style: observation in educational settings.

> As I recall, one thing that was really important to Miss Niebuhr was drama—used in its broadest sense.... One of our assignments was to attend the Christmas pageant at Fourth Presbyterian Church, because it was well done. We talked in class about how the people were chosen for the pageant, the personal preparation each had to make in order to get inside the character, the manner in which they performed.[57]

Another student recalled how Hulda read from books that she felt were appropriate for children and then would take off

> in delightful tangents related to her own experiences in working with children at [Madison Avenue] and at Boston U. How I'd love to hear her again! She was always pushing children's dramatics, helping children experience Biblical stories or ethical situations, rather than lecturing them or giving them the typical "children's sermons" with morals tacked on the end or with analogies children couldn't possibly understand. How she hated those children's sermons! When I hear them today (and they're still very much around), I cringe and think of Hulda.[58]

Another method Hulda taught to her students was storytelling. In her files are copies of stories written by students in her courses. Copies of these stories were shared with all members of a class, so that they would have a notebook of children's stories to use in their teaching. The stories written by students included the telling of stories of characters from the Bible as well as modern-day situations appropriate for the experience of children. In the preface of her book of stories, *Greatness Passing By*, Hulda said that an educational approach that "presumes to relate itself to life will use the story, for the story has its roots in life, it is life condensed, life in spot-light, it is of the essence of life itself…. When imagination is active in this way the hearer does not merely see things happen,—he feels them happen."[59]

Developing her students' skills in writing was also important to Hulda's purpose as a teacher. "She never lost an opportunity to challenge us to apply our skills in this area," a former student stated. "Indeed, when I was asked to write some units for Faith and Life Curriculum back in '58 and '59, I accepted the assignment because I felt her nudging me in that direction."[60] This concern with developing potential curriculum writers emerged after she had completed her book on the Bible for junior highs, *The One Story*, for the new Christian Faith and Life Curriculum of the Presbyterian Church, U.S.A., in 1948. It was the first venture for this denomination in writing and publishing its own material, and it was looking for future writers. In response to this need she handpicked

> ten of us to become a class in curriculum writing, at the conclusion of which she arranged for each of us to be put in contact with some of the editors of the curriculum. Out of that experience there developed for me a continuing opportunity to write for the Board for Junior and Senior High curriculum and for the Youth Kits.[61]

Hulda's purpose in each of these methods was to give students experience with teaching and learning activities that they would need to know in their work in educational ministry in the church. Experiential learning, as it is known today, probably would best describe her philosophy of education.

Hulda was concerned that her students not only know the method theoretically but that they have the opportunity to observe in an excellent educational setting, try it themselves, and share their attempts and struggles with their classmates for critique and evaluation of learning. This represents a holistic approach to learning involving the teacher and the learner as they engage together in the teaching and learning experience. What she modeled in her class as teacher was as important as what she taught.

> I remember so little of Miss Niebuhr's courses. I no longer have any of my McCormick notes, but I recall that none of us had many notes from Hulda's courses. There was no list of information to be written down and then memorized. Instead it was a matter of listening to her sweetness, her vast intelligence, her concern for humanity (particularly children), her liberal comments on our questions and our contributions—listening and catching her spirit.[62]

In pursuing questions about Hulda—what kind of teacher was she, what methods did she use in her classes, and what theories of learning informed her teaching—a further concept continues to emerge, that of the teacher as artist. In commenting on this one of her students, Robert Worley, said that "she gave a vision of what teaching should look like. The teacher as artist illustrates how she saw everything as having potential for learning: nature, art, drama, story, music. The teacher's role was to put reality together so that students could discover it and make it their own."[63]

Hulda Niebuhr spoke of the artist as teacher in the address she delivered at her inauguration as professor of Christian education at McCormick Theological Seminary on January 16, 1953.

> So the artist in the teacher sets forth in a context of life and activity whatever aspect of reality he is commending to his pupils and depends upon the pupil's intuitive conclusion, as that pupil takes hold of the quality of experience with the tentacles of his imagination, using then all his own conscious and pre-conscious knowledge, building up new structures of imagery, attended by sentiment and feeling.[64]

The question she sought to answer in that address was one that she believed offered the greatest challenge to the field of Christian education. "Is it possible that a Christian teacher of his religion can do more than merely tell and yet not indoctrinate?"[65]

She was also interested in comparing the teacher with the artist because she believed both obeyed a vision. Dissatisfied with dull and moralistic teaching, Hulda advocated for the kind of teacher who as an artist could enable a student to engage with reality not by telling about the subject but rather "make it come alive by leading into experience of that subject; and he [the teacher] expresses rather than describes what it means to him."[66] It was important that the teacher move beyond the act of telling. If this does not happen, she suggests the teacher "will not be able to stir another's imagination concerning a reality he himself has not seen, does not serve. Except as the love and the grace of God constrain and enable him, he cannot love his neighbor, his pupil, as himself."[67]

In many ways Hulda Niebuhr had the same expectations of learners as she had of teachers. Learners were expected to use their intuitions and creativity, to have a working mind. In the article "Learning by Heart—Then and Now," she contrasted rote learning and learning by heart. Hulda affirmed learning by heart on the part of the learner so that what was learned was "made a part of the warp and woof of being."[68] For Hulda, the teacher as artist was concerned with the whole fabric of faith as it related to everything the person did, inside and outside the classroom.[69]

Her students remember the methods she used in the classroom. "I knew then she was a pioneer in classroom involvement, and inter-relationships. No assignment was made in isolation from involvement. Students interacted with each other as well as with her. Everything was on a shared basis."[70] Another student, upon experiencing his first class with her, was not completely sure he would learn anything.

> I was very frustrated in the first class I took from her because the nature of her presentation was so different than my previous experience that I came away with very few notes. I was positive that I was going to learn nothing. On the contrary. Miss Niebuhr's method was to get us to do our own research and study; not to spoon-feed us. Her extensive outside reading requirements opened up a whole new world for me. Despite my lack of notes, I felt that I learned more in the process than in many other classes which I took.[71]

The clues to understanding Hulda Niebuhr's concept of the "teacher as artist" become more obvious. She was concerned with providing opportunities in class whereby students could not only experience what it meant to be a teacher but also to be responsible for shaping their own understanding or vision of their role as teacher. As one of her students has said,

> She insisted, to the dismay of many, that we each operate within an arena of responsible freedom. It was the freedom, not the responsibility, that vexed students accustomed to doing prescribed assignments step by step.... The few people I see often from those classes at McCormick say, "Miss Niebuhr was ahead of her time." She wasn't. The general public is behind the times.[72]

Hulda Niebuhr's emphasis on the "teacher as artist" and the activity of liberating the creativity of the pupil most probably reflect a synthesis of her theology and her understanding of human development as well as her training in educational theory. It is also very probable that her early experiences at home with the art and drama opportunities offered by her mother were formative in the development of her own philosophy of teaching and learning.

For Hulda Niebuhr, thinking about the Christian faith was not enough. Knowledge had to be translated into action. A praxis model of education expresses that theoretical thinking today. Translation of knowledge into action is one of the major theoretical concepts that make her thinking so applicable in the latter part of the twentieth century. Her concern with challenging nominal Christianity is an ever-recurring need of the church.

The danger of raising conventional Christians instead of spiritual progenitors is as much a pedagogical issue today as it was in Hulda Niebuhr's time. In her teaching, Hulda modeled what she taught about the artist as teacher.

Her mark was made in the classroom and in her relations with others. She had written to one of her former students about the magnum opus, the book she was writing on her philosophy of religious education. In her letters, she shared the outline of this book. After her death, Robert Worley and H. Richard Niebuhr went through her files searching for the magnum opus for which Worley had a publishing contract. The file folder was in the files but there was nothing in it. Her gifts as a teacher, which she communicated within the classroom rather than through the written word, are left only to those for whom she was a spiritual progenitor. Her students' memories confirm the artistic skill Hulda Niebuhr exhibited in maintaining the unity of the teacher's activity of being and doing.

LEGACY

The hymn sung just before Hulda Niebuhr's address during the service of her inauguration as professor on January 13, 1953, concluded with these words: "Lord God, whose grace has called us to thy service...we work with thee, we go where thou wilt lead us, until in all the earth Thy kingdom come."[73] Hulda's career had been one of service to God, journeying to places where her gifts as an educator could best be used by the church. The thirteen years she taught at McCormick Theological Seminary indicate the kinds of service that she offered and provide clues to the legacy she left in her role as a female faculty member, in her teaching, and in the contribution she made to community life on the McCormick Seminary campus.

The ambiguous status of a female colleague was of deep concern to Hulda. In a collection of her letters, there is an undated one to President Cotton that must have been written shortly after she arrived. Hulda raised a concern about a colleague, Ruth Bernice Mead, who was director of placement and supervisor of field work.

I have noticed that when notes go to the college faculty from the Seminary, Miss Mead's name is not included, but when a college faculty meeting is called it is assumed she is present. I seem to be thought of as the only woman faculty member on the campus, and that must make Miss Mead's position seem anomalous to her....I like her spirit and good intentions and think that if relationships were clearer I could be in better position to help the fine gifts, that seem partially submerged now by a sense of defeat, to be released for better service to the students and for sources of pleasure to herself.[74]

Hulda served as a role model of a woman faculty member. The journey to the McCormick faculty had involved a transition to a male, hierarchical, academic world. She was the first and the only female full professor in the seminary during her years there. Hulda taught mostly women before the college and the seminary were merged, but after the union her classes were more evenly divided between women seeking the master of arts in Christian education and men who were earning the three-year bachelor of divinity degree and seeking ordination as ministers. For many she was probably the first woman professor they had seen and the only one under whom they studied.

In the closing of a letter Hulda wrote to the president, she mentioned that on June 1946 at their Diamond Jubilee commencement, Elmhurst College would bestow on her an honorary doctor of literature degree. Consistent with her nature she concluded by saying, "I am not 'telling' that but thought you should know."[75]

When Hulda joined the faculty her committee assignments included the library and student/faculty benevolence. In later years she was also assigned to admissions, field work, senior placement, and the curriculum committees. After her inauguration as full professor with indeterminate tenure, Hulda was made a member of the educational policies and personnel committee, which was composed of faculty who were full professors. They were responsible for making recommendations to the president regarding faculty reviews and appointments and tenure. If one committee could be singled out as most powerful politically within the institution, this was it. Hulda served on this committee until her death.

Other than on such committees as field work and placement, Hulda was the only female voice represented on most of the committees on which she served during her years as a faculty member. There is no doubt that she was hired because of her ability and credentials as a church educator and as a teacher. She attained the rank of full professor at a time when those doors were mostly closed for women. It is possible to speculate that the Niebuhr name might have helped to open the doors for her as a woman who had not earned a doctorate. Yet she shared in her inauguration with a colleague, George-Williams Smith, who was also becoming a professor of speech. Like Hulda, his degrees were a master of arts and a doctor of literature. Hulda was sixty-four when she became a full professor, an age today when many professors are considering their future retirement rather than their future in teaching.

Hulda's contribution to McCormick in the area of theory and methods of teaching is clear from comments made by colleagues and students. It is a testimony to her skills and gifts that she was able to achieve a reputation as an excellent teacher in her field. During her years as a faculty member, a curriculum was in place that required ninety-six hours for graduation with the bachelor of divinity degree. Seventy-one of those hours were prescribed and twenty-five were available for electives. In the master of arts program, which offered specialization in religious education and social work, sixty-four hours of course work were required. Of those, two-thirds were prescribed and one-third were electives.

The curriculum structure was supported by a system of faculty hierarchy. Tenured professors taught the required courses, while the electives were left for junior faculty members. One professor who taught a required course in Christian education was described in this way.

> His notes were yellowed with age and really out of touch with the current educational trends. But with Hulda, you anxiously anticipated each class period with enthusiasm. Everything was fresh and new— Christian Education was an integral part of the life of the church scene and you were motivated to "make it happen."[76]

The other Christian education professor required class attendence and reading two thousand pages selected from the class bibliography. The dull lectures and unimaginative assignments so turned off students to the field that many never chose the elective courses in Christian education that were taught by Hulda. Hulda was very probably a victim of hierarchy, the hierarchy of a system that functioned to exclude newer faculty members from teaching courses in the required curriculum.

Thankfully many students were able to move beyond prescribed courses to experience Hulda's gifts as a teacher. Oscar Hussel, dean of academic affairs at Columbia Theological Seminary, was one of the many students in whom she invested herself and who she encouraged to continue study in the field of religious education.

> My lasting (and regularly confirmed by my own teaching experiences) impression of Miss Niebuhr is that she was the finest teacher I ever saw. A considerable amount of my understanding of the philosophy of education and of teaching methods I gained in her classes and in conversations. I must confess that I spent more time in class watching her teach than gaining knowledge of the subject matter. Her work in putting together religious education and then emerging ideas of general psychology and educational psychology opened up a new era in Christian education—one that is just now widely accepted in many congregations.[77]

Another student, Mary Duckert, took her curriculum writing course with Hulda Niebuhr seriously and went on to become a curriculum editor with the educational offices of the United Presbyterian Church U.S.A. In commenting on Hulda's teaching she said that "she espoused inductive teaching, discovery learning, original teaching plans and materials, and teacher/learner cooperative planning at a time when these ideas were understood and appreciated by a precious few and practiced by even fewer."[78] In an article she wrote for a denominational magazine, Duckert gave a memorable example.

> She was thoroughly steeped in research findings in child development over a long period of years. I remember seeing in class an old length of film from Dr. Gesell's early research, the findings of which were alluded to in an interview with a psychiatrist about a year ago. Hulda Niebuhr provided the opportunity for me to learn from that research, but she was not the originator. Many knew what she knew and what she taught, but most did not.[79]

When former students have been asked to comment on her teaching methods, they find it difficult to separate what she taught from who she was.

> My overall recollection of Hulda Niebuhr is that of a mystical person, one whose very life styles spoke with authority without being authoritarian, spoke eloquently, verbally and non-verbally about the mysteries of God and the service of the church. All of this is coupled with the tremendous sense of humor and humanness.[80]

Another said that "she was an Andrew, introducing her kind to the Word Incarnate, and watching them learn and do from the encounter."[81] The reference is most likely to Andrew, one of the Twelve Disciples of Jesus. What this student experienced was a teacher who provided the context and the resources with which students could learn and then expected students to be responsible for their own learning. "She was always in the background. It amazes me that she has become as memorable as she has. I suspect without the publicized and published brothers, she may indeed have belonged only to those who appreciated and learned from her at McCormick."[82]

The years that Hulda and her mother lived on the McCormick Seminary campus evidenced a dramatic transformation in social relationships. Essential in identifying that transformation is the role that Lydia Niebuhr played and her relationship to the community. As in each situation when she made a move with one of her children, Lydia wasted no time in discovering the special contribution she could make to the life of the community in which she found herself. Her ability to adapt herself to each of these environments was a gift and a remarkable talent. She was seventy-five when she made the move to Chicago. Hulda described her mother's contribution in this way:

> Mother has been very active on Chalmers Place, our faculty row. When she sits on the porch, weather permitting, there are always faculty and students and other neighbor children about. When there is no school or they are for any reason looking for something to engage their interest, they come asking, "What can we do today?" On the day before Christmas they gave her a birthday surprise at a neighbor's home, some thirty of them. Knowing Mother's interest in the things children make, they each brought something of their own creation.[83]

Hulda went on to describe how her mother's art activities went well beyond the boundaries of the campus. Students who had field work assignments in settlement houses and churches in Chicago would bring groups of children to the Niebuhr home to learn blueprinting, stained glass, or shell art with Lydia as their teacher.

> One sixth grade day school class became interested in stained glass windows when they were studying medieval history. A friend of the teacher told them of Mother's interest . . . and they came to our house in groups of five or six until all had taken part in making a stained glass composition. They had one for each window in their classroom. The children then planned a party in Mother's honor and presented her with a new electric soldering iron, believing that they had pretty well worn out the one she had used with them.[84]

In an article he wrote on Lydia for a denominational magazine, Ralph Abele, a former assistant pastor with Reinhold at Bethel Evangelical Church described the Niebuhr home as "partly study, partly hobby work-shop, and always a rendezvous for children and students."[85]

Two activities started by Lydia quickly became McCormick traditions.

> There are two parades here yearly on Chalmers Place which Mother has organized with the children, a Memorial day one called the "Everything on Wheels Parade," followed by a program of the children's planning with Mother and picnic supper on the green, the families of faculty, students, neighbors taking part. Another parade is being called by now a McCormick tradition. In the fall, as soon as darkness comes early enough and before it is too cold, there is a so called "Lighthouse" parade, big and smaller boxes with windows

covered with colored paper lights inside.... The students furnish an orchestra, rather a band, to precede the children.[86]

The tradition of the "wheel parade" continued until very recently on the old McCormick campus. On the occasion of her last "wheel parade" before her move from the campus, Lydia was honored by the community. "It'll be Mrs. Niebuhr's Day" was the headline of the newspaper article that included a picture of Lydia standing with some children, her "other family" as the article identified them. "Children feel it if you love them. They have made my life rich," Lydia was quoted as saying.[87] This activity provided a way for the community to say thank-you and good-bye to one whom they had known as family.

THREADS OF A LIFE

The extent to which Hulda gave of herself to her teaching, writing, and work with students meant that twice she required time from the seminary in order to restore her health. Rev. June K. Stansbery recalled that Hulda was given a sabbatical to recover her voice that she had lost when "pushed so hard to write the Christian Faith and Life Curriculum book, *The One Story*. She was warned not to talk for six months and could not teach the first semester I was at the Presbyterian College of Christian Education."[88] In a letter to the president of McCormick, Worth Frank, Hulda commented on this time of rest and recovery.

Some people...in continued times of pressure, will use up their eyes, the heart, the digestive tract. My deficit showed in my throat. I have to learn, it appears, to throw any pressure I may feel, on some organ I don't happen to be using at the time. I have not yet decided which one that is to be.... I really have to learn to be relaxed all over, deadlines or no. I will see what I can do about that, only I know my short-comings.... My brothers write much advice about relaxing, using the time for refreshment of all sorts, with P S "Don't fret, whatever you do." If I take all the advice to that effect I may get so lazy it will be hard to start again.[89]

In January of 1959, just prior to her planned retirement, Hulda and her mother both became ill. The seminary worked to protect Hulda's health by scheduling courses opposite her course in "Adolescence" in order to keep the enrollment down. "Anything we can do to make the load at the house easier, such as helping the students to become accustomed to dropping you notes rather than dropping themselves in your living room, we will do."[90]

Hulda responded to Arthur McKay, president of McCormick Theological Seminary from 1958 to 1970, with appreciation for the help he had extended. She concluded with these words: "Mother is on the mend and I, too, can be conscious of real progress the last week or ten days. I do not feel any more that faith will be needed to remove mountains,—just some hills."[91]

Hulda had obviously suggested that in light of a reduction of her responsibilities that some adjustment in her salary was in order. She had made this same offer when she had been sick in 1948. McKay responded to her:

> Your passing reference in the hallway to any salary adjustment because of your lighter course load was most gracious. In my judgment that matter needs no further consideration.... We are on entirely sound ground in terms of compensation, especially in view of the fact that we have never overpaid you in any of your years of service here at the Seminary.[92]

McKay also corresponded with H. Richard about Hulda and Lydia's health, keeping the family informed about the administration's care for two especially important and loved members of the seminary community.

Hulda Niebuhr died at age seventy on April 17, 1959. The next letter in the seminary president's file is the announcement of her death that was posted for the community. Her health had continued to deteriorate, and she went for an appointment to her doctor's office, where she died of a heart attack. The community quietly and quickly sustained Lydia and her family as they dealt with this unexpected death. The outpouring and warmth of care extended to Lydia, who was then ninety years old, and to her sons upon the death of Hulda was not a token response but a genuine expression of grief.

Hulda's last thirteen years provided her with the opportunity to integrate the threads that added color and texture to her life. Her writing, her mentoring activity, and her role as community builder exemplified the values and beliefs that she learned early in life.

The environment of the McCormick campus provided a hospitable community in which Hulda and her mother could be nurtured and cared for as family. They were initiators of community on the campus as well as recipients of the resultant warmth of caring, personal relationships. In a letter to Reinhold after Hulda's death, President McKay indicated these feelings.

> My thoughts and prayers have often been with you during these past two weeks. Hulda's death came as a great blow to us all. Loving and

respecting her as we did, we know something of the depth of bereavement which Mütterkind, Richard, and yourself feel.[93]

The sense of community that Hulda and Lydia shared at McCormick was also the experience of Reinhold and H. Richard. Reinhold expressed his gratitude to McCormick and to the faculty "whose friendship made the life of my mother and sister so happy.... They spent the happiest days of their lives at McCormick."[94]

After Lydia's death on January 24, 1961 in Lincoln, Illinois, H. Richard wrote President McKay giving his thanks for "the warm, friendly, family-like environment" that the seminary provided for his mother.

> She was attached to McCormick in a unique way; felt safe and secure with you as I believed she had not felt since her widowhood began. Reinie and I are deeply sensible of the good you did here in her life-time and feel a kind of personal kinship to your seminary because of it.[95]

Having visited his family on the McCormick campus over the years, H. Richard had experienced firsthand the warmth of the seminary and appreciated the sustaining presence of a caring, faithful community during his grief over the death of his mother.

> But I have my own particular sense of gratitude, too, as one who was there and for whom the presence of mother's friends and my McCormick friends was a source of strength and consolement. They took good care of one who is old enough to take care of himself but so young still that he is easily left desolate.[96]

Lydia's estate left money for the memorial fund established in memory of her daughter. In addition, royalties from Hulda's book *The One Story* were left to McCormick. In conversation with H. Richard, it was decided that the memorial fund would be used in designing a teaching room as a part of the library development project. In a letter to H. Richard, President McKay said that "within the proposed new library there are two kinds of rooms which will be in regular use for instructional purposes that reflect some of Hulda's deepest convictions about the way in which learning takes place."[97]

So the threads of intellectual ability, a faith visible in ways of being and doing, and a gift for empowering the strengths of others were woven in rich colors in Hulda's service to McCormick Theological Seminary. The strength of these threads is no surprise since they were ones whose weaving had begun in her childhood. The threads continue to serve as Hulda's legacy to those who would aspire to be spiritual progenitors for others.

Hulda in her final years, c. 1959

5

Claiming Great Freedom

A NIEBUHR FESTIVAL, TO HONOR the contribution of Reinhold and H. Richard, was held at Eden Seminary in April 1979. Joan Beebe, a member of the faculty at the time, asked if Hulda was to be included in the celebration. The response was, "Who is Hulda?" Hulda was included in the festival because Joan Beebe researched the subject and presented a paper, "Hulda Niebuhr, A Light for Christian Education." This was probably the first public recognition of Hulda's contribution to the field of religious education beyond that given at her memorial service at McCormick Theological Seminary.

It is true that by traditional standards of academic success Hulda Niebuhr did not achieve prominence as an educational leader. Her publications were slight, including only three books and nine journal articles. What could have been a lasting contribution to the history of religious education theory was never published. Indeed, no evidence that the book was ever written was found.

The life of Clara Augusta Hulda Niebuhr was significant, however, to the history of women, to the history of the Niebuhr family, and to religious education. What were the qualities that enabled her to serve as a pioneering role model for other women following their vocational dreams?

PERSONAL SIGNIFICANCE

A reflection on Hulda Niebuhr's life provides an opportunity to consider why this particular woman is significant. She was able successfully to individuate from her family and claim her identity and voice. Her role model had been set for her. She was to emulate her mother and work as a tireless parish assistant; or she was to follow in the path of her aunt, Adele Hosto, and serve the church as a deaconess. Though equal partners with her brothers in the academic and artistic environment of the Niebuhr home, less was expected of Hulda because she was female. "Early on Hulda showed academic promise. In Lincoln High School, she was on the honor roll and was secretary of the literary society, the Adelphians."[1] Her father assumed that "good girls didn't need or want university training."[2] Chrystal makes clear this curious anomaly in Gustav's reaction to his gifted daughter. "Although Gustav Niebuhr had been offended by the way his own father had treated his mother, he saw nothing wrong with keeping Hulda from attending college. This he no doubt believed would make her a better marriage prospect for an educated young man."[3]

Obviously for Hulda's father, a woman's education was utilitarian in purpose, not for her benefit but for its usefulness in a woman's support of her husband. Gustav watched as his daughter took independent steps on her own journey in spite of his dogmatic position and began her college education. With quiet yet firm determination, Hulda chose to take her future into her own hands rather than leave it to the chance of a yet unknown "educated young man."

Hulda's life is also significant in her ability to separate from her mother, who she was to emulate. Both possessed strong personalities, Lydia's more extroverted than Hulda's. From that perspective they seem to complement each other, sharing a love for teaching, for working with children, and for enabling creative, artistic abilities to emerge in people.

Hulda never seemed overwhelmed by living in the shadow of famous brothers. To her they were just that, her brothers. She enjoyed sharing her family with the McCormick Seminary community when its members came for visits. Neither was Hulda overwhelmed by her mother's need for leadership in areas that overlapped her own, including teaching at Madison Avenue Presbyterian Church and working with children on the McCormick campus. The complementary role they shared served to sustain them. Lydia was housekeeper for Hulda, cooking the meals and sewing her clothes. Hulda helped to provide the receptive environment and the contact with children that made their home open and hospitable.

Hulda was able to establish her identity as a Niebuhr woman. As one of her former students, Oscar Hussel, has said, "She was . . . in my opinion, equal in ability and insight with her brothers. If they were in their career today with the new value granted to women, I am sure she would be far more widely known and respected."[4] Being widely known and respected was not necessary for Hulda's individuating process, but claiming her own voice was essential to whom she was as a woman and as a professional.

In her soft-spoken yet determined ways, Hulda challenged the notion of separate spheres that sought to limit women's search for equality in professions. The time when she began her work as a college student in 1912 and again in 1919 was one of relative freedom for women, "especially in giving them a more open-ended sense of their own capacities."[5] The battles, to prove the incorrectness of the belief that education for women would harm their minds and bodies, had been waged, won, and laid to rest. Slowly the culture grew to accept that the home was not the limit of a woman's world.[6]

The world Hulda entered, however, was still confused about the appropriateness of professions for women. This was demonstrated within her family. Though her father's determined position seemed to be based on a woman losing her femininity, the culture grew increasingly concerned with its own feminization caused by a shift in the balance of power that had traditionally been weighted toward males.[7]

Hulda, once her educational and career goals became identified, moved ahead with her life, determined to prepare for a profession for which she believed she was well suited. In some ways, she was like another pioneer in her day, Marion Talbot, dean at the University of Chicago in 1892. Hulda's life "provided a bridge, linking an older view of feminine uniqueness to a more modern view of woman's uncharted potential."[8]

The home and church were the two acceptable spheres for women in the latter part of the nineteenth century. The limits of these spheres for women, combined with the dominant Niebuhr family profession, served to focus Hulda's vision of her vocational future. The profession that Hulda chose, church educator, is often described today as a woman's field, only one step removed from the home. In her day, however, the vocation of church educator was an acceptable career path for both women and men. Boston University's School of Religious Education and Social Service, during Hulda's time there, was a place of equality for female and male students. "By the 1920's it was no longer unusual for men to attend graduate school; but it remained unusual for women, for whom graduate education never achieved a corresponding social utility."[9]

In this sense, then, Hulda pioneered as a woman who pursued higher education, leading to a career in teaching and administration. The social utility of her work provided Hulda with the necessary experience that enabled her to critique her learning. She intentionally envisioned the kind and shape of future academic studies she would need to successfully bridge the transition between theory and practice.

When Marion Talbot was leaving Wellesley College to become dean of the University of Chicago, her friends gave her gifts of dishes and linens, preferring to view her move "as a kind of marriage.... In 1892, women who challenged conventional views of feminine capacity usually found they had to do so alone."[10]

When Hulda Niebuhr gave notice to Madison Avenue Presbyterian Church that she would be leaving to accept a position on the faculty at the Presbyterian College of Christian Education in Chicago, she made it clear that she would remain in New York for six months to honor her teaching commitment at New York University and to spend some time in study and writing. The congregation responded with a monetary gift that enabled her to be financially independent during her sabbatical quarter. The difference in the parting gifts to these two women illustrates the steps, although small ones, that women were able to make in claiming their place in a culture determined to limit the spheres of their vocations.

Hulda served as an important role model for women in challenging hierarchical academic practices. McCormick was typical of Protestant seminaries in its treatment of women. From its origin in Hanover, Indiana, in 1829, it had been a school for male students. In 1927, after its move to Chicago, the first women's rest rooms were installed in McCormick's buildings. Women had been accepted as students as early as 1918. It was not until 1948, however, that the first woman was allowed to receive the bachelor of divinity degree.

The discussion of the merger of the Presbyterian College of Christian Education and McCormick Theological Seminary began with a set of "Articles of Affiliation" in 1944. The faculty of McCormick, supporting the idea of cooperation, began by listing the college and seminary faculty and courses in the same catalog. Since the college's academic entrance requirements were equivalent to the seminary's, both schools were graduate institutions. Obviously the fear of feminization of a male institution was more than the faculty could abide, evidenced in their vote in 1945 to deny the women of the college the privilege of eating their meals in the Commons, the dining facility on the seminary campus.[11]

Such was the situation into which Hulda moved in 1946. Her single-minded pursuit of equitable treatment as a faculty member and her expectation of recognition for her abilities as a competent teacher and scholar gave notice to McCormick that she would not only find her place as the first woman to be a full professor within the faculty but would pave the way for other women to follow.

Hulda Niebuhr serves as a role model for leaders in the field of religious education, even today, who seek to integrate theory and practice. Consistent in comments from her students is an awareness of how different her teaching was from the traditional academic model of the teacher as an expert whose goal was to open the student's head and pour in information. In reflecting on her teaching style, students provide evidence that the lecture method was a predominant pedagogical method used at McCormick.

Hulda started from a different context in her model of teaching and learning. The content of the course, the process of learning, and the knowledge and abilities of the students were held together in a dynamic tension. She expected more of her students than listening and taking notes. Hulda valued a working mind that could reflect on the content and its relationship to the practice of educational ministry.

Hussel recalls this memory of Hulda Niebuhr as a teacher:

It becomes obvious that the form and spirit that Hulda discussed in class, the "warp and woof" of being, were not merely lectures for her but a lifestyle. She was a gentle and kind person who (in addition to her high professional skills) cared about her students. I remember her knocking on the door of the Hussel apartment in McCormick Hall and giving me a plate of cookies to share with my wife, just back from the hospital. (Being a pastor to pupils). It is not enough to know your pupils; you must love them also.[12]

Hulda also contributed to an understanding of the person of the female teacher. Her identity as a single, professional woman included a philosophy of caring and responsibility to her students and to her work. Hulda and Lydia were major contributors to a new style of community life on campus that bridged the time between the formality of calling cards, white gloves, and afternoon teas to the time of seminary and neighborhood community parades and celebrations on the campus. Luella Cotton, wife of President Harry Cotton, commented on this contribution of the Niebuhr women.

She [Hulda] and her mother were warmly accepted and both added to the seminary community. I know she was asked to be on the faculty because of her own abilities and her record in Christian education altho there was always that question: "Is she the sister of..." etc. But she did not shine, in reflection of them—she had attained her right to shine.[13]

The significance of Hulda's teaching centers upon the relationship between the theory and practice of religious education. Her theory had been tested out in her life experiences, beginning with her leadership in her father's church in Lincoln, Illinois. Hulda succeeded in her goal in moving beyond "talking out of notebooks." Her years at McCormick reveal a professional woman whose philosophy of religious education was not written between the pages of a book. Rather it was written clearly in her class sessions, her advising of students, her assignments to visit Juvenile Court, settlement houses, and local congregations, and in her journal articles and books for children and teachers.

Hulda's significance lies in her choice to invest herself in her teaching and in her students. Her research and her writing were important to her. More important, however, she made her mark in the world by educating women and men who would possess the educational abilities to serve the church and the world with a vision for God's realm.

ORIGINS OF HER MATURE THEORY

Hulda Niebuhr's theory of religious education, which can be inferred from her teaching and writing, was the result of a lifelong process of learning. The evolution of her theory and practice of religious education began at home with the instruction, both formal and informal, that she received from her parents. Hulda was not a disciple of any one particular school of thinking concerning her theory of religious education. Her theory was woven from the threads of her experience as a child in the German Evangelical Niebuhr home, in her academic studies, in her work as a religious educator, and in her teaching. These threads are essential to understanding the tapestry of her theory.

Lydia's contribution to an Evangelical perspective included these essential tenets: (1) the Bible is the Word of God that can be understood by children, young people, and adults when taught with appropriate methods of instruction; (2) faith is concerned with the way a person lives and is related to others; and (3) faith is a concern of both the church and the home and cannot be expected to grow without instruction and experience during the week as well as on Sunday. Hulda thus inherited from her parents both theology and methodology that were foundational to her developing theory of religious education.

Hulda's book *The One Story* shows how her theology and her theory of religious education were woven together. Written for junior-high-age youth, this book was a part of the Christian Faith and Life Curriculum of the United Presbyterian Church U.S.A. used in the late 1940s and 1950s. *The One Story* tells the biblical story as a consecutive narrative, demonstrating how God's relationship with humankind is really one story. Hulda's intention was to show how

> again and again man rebelled against God. His pride was great, and he thought the way to be truly happy was to do just as he pleased. So God set about winning man to himself. The story of how he did it is the one great story of the Bible.[14]

In telling the biblical story using modern language, Hulda provided a creative way for adolescents to engage in biblical study. Skilled as a storyteller, Hulda was able to show how the stories in both the Old and New Testaments were intimately related to each other and to the present reality of young people living in the twentieth century.

It was consistent with Hulda's role as a teacher that she served as mentor for her students. She believed it was important to challenge her students to think, to create, and to envision their role as educators with congregations. Hulda's commitment to the educing, leading out activity of education showed her awareness that theological students had particular gifts for leadership in the field of religious education.

Some students worked with Hulda toward the master of arts degree with a major in Christian education. Others worked on this degree with her after completing a bachelor of divinity degree. Hulda's students found their places for ministry as church educators, pastors, church executives, school teachers, curriculum writers and editors, seminary professors, and deans. Her mentoring provided the challenge and personal care that were qualities she believed to be essential for ministry.

In "A Room of One's Own," Virginia Wolff described the feminist process of "thinking back through our mothers." Such a process invites women

> to recollect, to re-collect the process of our own formation.... We have access, paths of feeling, of memory, into the gardens where our first worlds grew. That is the soil we need to turn over, as we study the relations within which subject and object, parent and child, ego and ego, persona and world, come to form.[15]

In her process of individuation, Hulda did not have to become like her mother. Yet her development did include "thinking back through her mother" in order to claim her own ways of seeing and understanding herself as a teacher. Madeleine Grumet has said that "stigmatized as 'women's work,' teaching rests waiting for us to reclaim it and transform it into the work of women."[16] Hulda was an active voice in both the process of reclamation and transformation of the vocation of teaching.

Sources for determining Hulda's theory of religious education are the published articles she wrote from 1933 to 1959. For Hulda Niebuhr, Christian education was "the believing community at work helping people listen and look in order that by God's grace they may hear and see and so be helped to know the hope to which they are called by God in Jesus Christ."[17] The nature of Christian education was concerned with the church as faith community and with individuals and their relationship with God.

In an article, "Red Roses and Sin," Hulda commented on how "we bemoan the fact that our church members do not know the Bible, while at the same time we waste opportunities to make it available to them."[18] She went on to talk about the use of drama and stories that "will capture the imagination, interpret the biblical text, and open the doors of faith to the children."[19] Though talking about children, her purpose in religious education is clearly also appropriate for all ages in the church.

In stating her purpose of Christian education, Hulda said,

> It is the task of Christian Education to furnish imaginations with the story of salvation so that it may become a part of each individual's own history, absorbed into the context of his own particular life, be he young or older, rich or poor, from east or west.[20]

It was essential for Hulda to maintain a tension between the imagination of the learner, the appropriation of the Christian faith, and the appreciation of faith in individual lives.

For Hulda, the content of religious education was both the biblical story and present life situations. She could begin with either as content but was always concerned with both and with the way in which the Bible informed a person's practice of religious faith. In "Trying on Life," she described a study by junior high boys of the topic "Being Neighbors" based on Romans 15:5–7. The passage came to have real meaning for the group when the boys were first involved in role plays and then in visiting youth in the neighborhood to invite them to church. Another example of her blending of these ideas is evidenced in her article "Thanksgiving for Our Time," written in 1933.

Obviously one could not, in these times celebrate Thanksgiving by singing "For Peace and for Plenty."…Fruits and grain enough there were, to be sure, but not peace exactly, and surely not plenty. What might be an honest Thanksgiving celebration for a group of junior and intermediate girls and boys many of whom lacked so greatly of the things they might reasonably desire?…This Thanksgiving celebration, therefore, might be the occasion to come to grips with the age-long "problem of evil." At least it might be possible to work out an approach to it.[21]

The role of the teacher was clearly defined by Hulda. A teacher was to be involved in confronting pupils with the meaning of the gospel in imaginative ways and was to be aware of the circumstances in which they lived. Two ideas that more clearly capture Hulda's understanding of the role of the teacher are the teacher as guardian and guide and the teacher as artist.

In "The Teacher's Authority" she compared the freedom of the pupil with the authority of the teacher. By freedom of the pupil Hulda meant the teacher's affirmation of the students' abilities to make choices, "aliveness, purpose and activity close to the heart of the pupil, meaningful to him, issuing in thought, insight, understanding, experiences which are the people's own and not merely echoes and repetitions."[22] The teacher served as a guide to pupils so that such experiences could be available to them.

In her understanding of the teacher as artist, Hulda was committed to educing the way that the teacher acted

to help the pupil make the gospel experience his own, its historic context invading the pupil's own, so that the pupil can live in that context, can snare it in imagination and discover for himself its meaning. As believer, the teacher is part of a community that lives in response to God's claim upon it, teaching of God's grace, probably unconscious of the fact that any teaching is going on.[23]

She believed that it was important for teachers to enable their students to discover their own truths about God. "As Christian the teacher is helped by the experience of life under God as a succession of acts of growth."[24]

And as mentioned earlier, Hulda expected learners to think actively, to use their intuitions and creativity, to learn by heart so that what is learned becomes part of the person's very being, one's "warp and woof."[25]

The context of the teaching and learning situation was very important to Hulda. She believed that the environment embodied a teacher's care, intention, planning, and understanding of the age group. The context of teaching also extended far beyond the classroom walls or even the walls of the church building itself. In response to a request for children to be involved in giving money for the restoration of the building, Hulda described a teacher who involved her pupils

> in their own investigation of the conditions of the church building. Their research resulted in an active and excited campaign to raise an amount the pupils set for themselves as a goal, higher than their leaders would have expected, and they raised it.[26]

In reflecting on Hulda's theory of religious education, it is obvious that she was influenced by developmental theory. Understanding of children and youth and their developmental growth as a basis for educational planning was fundamental to her work. Her concern for children, as in her article "Know Them as Persons," focuses on the child as learner, a major issue for progressive educators. For Hulda, teaching was more than simple moralizing and more than rote or dull learning. Creative education was at the heart of her method. Dramatic play as a way of "trying on life" was one means she frequently used herself and recommended to her students.[27] Storytelling was another method she believed would help children use their imagination in relating the Christian faith to daily life.

In attempting to identify the theology supporting Hulda's theory, it becomes clear that her thinking was a product of her background in the Evangelical church. God was understood as creator, redeemer, and judge. The church was conceived as a Christian community, a redemptive fellowship. Both the freedom and the responsibility of human beings was affirmed as well as their need of salvation by grace through faith. Hulda believed that the Bible was the Word of God and was concerned that it not be studied superficially but with enthusiasm and as a source of guidance for life. Her hope was that through teaching and learning in the church, students would "come to know the Christian community as a redemptive fellowship where each takes up a cross in love for and obedience to the God of our Lord Jesus Christ, who is both judge and redeemer, not an easy-going God."[28]

GAINING VOICE

Hulda lived during an era when the intelligence, abilities, and leadership of women were gaining slow acceptance in the culture. Still, the fields of education in general and religious education in particular were ones into which women were welcomed and encouraged.

In establishing herself as a single, professional woman, Hulda had to confront three impediments: her family, cultural assumptions about women, and institutions. The most outstanding familial restraint to her unique identity and independent voice was her father and his firmly held convictions about women's education and its negative impact on women and families.

Cultural expectations for women in the first few decades of the twentieth century were still focused on the woman's role as wife and mother. Educational barriers had begun to come down, but academic studies didn't offer the same professional opportunities for women as they did for men. Patriarchal and hierarchical employment practices were powerful indicators of cultural assumptions. In academic institutions women were more in evidence as assistant professors, instructors, and lecturers than as full professors.

Hulda eventually assumed the title of associate director of religious education at Madison Avenue Presbyterian Church. She most likely helped oversee the work of the women who were employed as assistant directors of religious education. She also worked with one of the ministers in supervising seminary students in their field education placements from Union Theological Seminary. In the fifteen years that she worked there, Hulda never achieved the title of director. It was always held by a male. Some of the same institutional practices were in place at McCormick Theological Seminary and the Presbyterian College of Christian Education, where she was originally offered the position of instructor in children's work.

Such impediments are visible in hindsight to the biographer looking through the lens of a feminist critique. To Hulda, they were perceived as impediments, never obstacles around which she could not maneuver.

The impetus for her individuation and claiming of voice found its sources in her family, the church, her colleagues and friends, and her students. Her father made it difficult for her to move ahead with her own intellectual pursuits. In the partnership of father and mother, however, Gustav and Lydia provided the kind of home that stimulated and encouraged intellectual maturity.

Hulda knew that she was an intelligent woman possessing abilities as an artist, teacher, and administrator.[29] The churches where her father and brother Reinhold served as pastors were communities that accepted and appreciated Hulda's gifts as teacher and leader. She was sustained early in her life by her family and by her faith communities.[30]

Also important in confirming her abilities as an educator were Hulda's teachers and colleagues at Boston University. Entering as an undergraduate, Hulda was quickly asked to maintain a balance between the roles of student and teacher when she was employed in the weekday school. Her teachers recognized her abilities and expected her to live up to her potential. Such expectations seemed to reinforce her confidence and motivated her to pursue further graduate study.

Life with students on the McCormick campus further served as a driving force in helping Hulda to establish her presence within that community. Comments from students about Hulda focus equally on her teaching style in class and on her caring relationship with them outside class, both of which served as major contributions to the McCormick community academically, pastorally, and socially. Hulda found in her students, as their teacher and as a caring adult, a recognition of her gifts as an educator and a leader and the power of her quiet yet authoritative voice.

To uncover the pedagogical style of a leader in the field of religious education is a difficult historical task when most primary sources preserved by institutions are texts and inaugural addresses. Men who were colleagues in Hulda's day wrote about their philosophy of religious education, not their pedagogical style.

A recent forum focused on the contribution of three women to the teaching of religious education at Union Theological Seminary: Sophia Fahs, Mary Tully, and Hulda Niebuhr. What became obvious in their stories was the spirit of their being and the experience-centered orientation of their teaching styles. In each case the biographer telling the story had been a student of the woman or had relied on stories from students to describe the pedagogical style.[31]

Hulda Niebuhr can be described as a maternal thinker who sought to make her classroom a connected one, where learners were intentional partners in the teaching and learning process.[32] Students have commented on her nonjudgmental teaching style. She was also described as authoritative, a person who expected her students to be responsible members of the community of learning she was seeking to establish. "Know your pupils was one of her favorite affirmations."[33] She knew her students through class discussions, assignments, papers, visits in her home, and consultations in her office.

> She was the most creative person and teacher I ever had and was the person who forced me to use my own creative talents and get away from a formal printed lesson plan. I'll never forget her accompanying me to my Sunday field work to see me teach and then the loving way she counseled me afterward.[34]

Hulda exemplified the connected teaching model of confirmation-evocation-confirmation, a cycle of learning that affirmed the learner's experience yet invited the student to move beyond. "In Miss Niebuhr's classes one was never finished altogether. The last assignment in each course was to write a short essay called 'Next Steps.'"[35]

Teaching the whole person was of primary concern to Hulda. She modeled for her students what she expected of them—holding in creative tension the importance of the head and the heart. At her memorial service in the chapel on the McCormick Seminary campus, her skill as a teacher was affirmed.

> Into all of her teaching she put intelligent and helpful Christian concern for the life of the Church and the growth of her students....Professor Niebuhr gave dignity and distinction to the calling of the teacher. It sounds trite to say that she was interested in her students; we have always sensed that fact in all that she said and did; but none the less that interest was a great and life-shaping fact. She discerned the weaknesses and limitations of her students, but her friendship and her appreciation of their possibilities open to them the way of growth and Christian usefulness.[36]

A RELUCTANT PIONEER

In reflecting on Hulda Niebuhr's life, it is possible to say that she was a pioneer, serving as an important role model for women who would follow her journey as a religious educator and professor. But she seemed a reluctant pioneer.

Hulda was reluctant to publish. The two books she had suggested she was working on before her arrival at McCormick in 1946, one on children and worship and the other on her philosophy of religious education, were never completed. Both books would have made significant contributions to the theory and practice of religious education. The perspective on such theory and practice from one such as Hulda, who had experience both as an educator in congregations and as a professor, would have added a unique contribution to a field dominated by academic theoreticians.

George Albert Coe, Sophia Fahs, Harrison Sackett Elliott, Randolph Crump Miller, Lewis Sherrill, James Smart, Sara Little, and C. Ellis Nelson are recognized as leaders in the field of Protestant religious education in the 1940s and 1950s. It would be easier to advocate for Hulda's inclusion with these leaders if she had been more intentional in making her voice heard through her writing. Limiting her publishing from 1946 to 1959 to six journal articles, one curriculum resource for the United Presbyterian Church U.S.A., and ten articles for the alumni bulletin of McCormick Theological Seminary insured her anonymity.

If the empty file thought to contain her magnum opus had been full instead of empty, Hulda's perspective on the theory and practice of religious education would have been left as a significant work for critique of the field during this era. Whether conscious or unconscious, Hulda chose to make the relational activities with her students, her family, and those with whom she worked in the church and the seminary the priority for her time and energy.

Hulda was also reluctant to speak loudly, making explicit her methodology. "There was a clear experiential dimension to her teaching—for instance we observed family court and talked afterward with attorneys, social workers and the judge in regard to their perspectives on youth and their needs."[37] The method Hulda used to integrate knowledge with reflection and critique of readings, class discussions, and experiential educational opportunities was intentionally chosen to enable students to make transitions between the theory and practice of religious education.

Consistent with a praxis model of education, Hulda began with a focus on the learner. Rosalie W. Mixon, the widow of one of Hulda's colleagues, commented on Hulda's method:

> Hulda and John [Mixon] were close friends and discussed at length the type of education that would benefit students most.... Hulda was very realistic in her conception of Christian education. She had a view of education that was progressive for her day.[38]

Hulda's practice of this method was certainly intentional, based on years of observation of and experience working with lay persons, educators, and ministers in the congregations with whom she was associated. In reflecting on their experiences with Hulda as their teacher, students are clearly able to identify her method and to observe that it was different from those of her colleagues.

Hulda evidently did not believe it was important to articulate publicly her method of teaching or to assert its relevance for theological education. Her failure to speak loudly, to use any written pieces, such as journal articles, for reflecting on the nature of teaching religious education using an experiential learning method, has left a void in understanding the history of the development of teaching in the field of religious education.

Finally, Hulda was reluctant to present herself as an authority. This was consistent with her personality and with her method of teaching and learning. She is remembered as a teacher who never imposed herself on her students but rather made possible opportunities for learning.

> I do not remember a lot of lectures. I do remember that she provided a wide range of experiences, projects and resources, which we

undertook and shared. There was no question about her authority and expertise, but she seemed to be in the role of a fellow learner.[39]

The comment about Hulda being "in the role of a fellow learner" is revealing in its perception, particularly when juxtaposed with the description of her "authority and expertise." Hulda's authority was captured in quieter, less explicit ways than her colleagues.

Students, accustomed to authoritarian lectures, would sometimes experience frustration in Hulda's refusal to claim authority by telling them what to think. Hulda Niebuhr was reluctant to present herself as an authority using traditional academic methods. Hulda's refusal to conform to this norm means that she was probably described as a practitioner rather than an academic. She doubtlessly would have debated the appropriateness of the conceptualization of those roles.

The question remains, was her voice really lost? The answer is both no and yes. Her voice is alive in the memories of students who recall not only the content of her instruction but also her methods of teaching and learning. Thirty years after taking her courses, some students are still able to recall vividly her talents and gifts as a teacher.

Yes, till now, her philosophy of religious education, her teaching methods, and her contribution to knowledge about the history of the teaching of religious education in theological institutions have been a lost voice. Hulda was not concerned with leaving her legacy in a written form.

During the last few years of her life, Hulda was focused on her teaching, her administrative responsibilities, the health of her mother, and her own physical limitations. Though hers was a strong voice, there was not enough heart left to complete the magnum opus that she had envisioned as her major contribution to thinking about religious education. The "empty file" is perhaps a strong symbol for the heart Hulda lost in her commitment to leaving a written legacy. Her life journey really involved holding heart and voice together. The history of the field would be enriched if Hulda Niebuhr had added her perspective, sharing her wealth of knowledge with those who were to follow in her footsteps.

A CLOUD OF WITNESSES

In his foreword to Chrystal's biography of Gustav Niebuhr, Richard R. Niebuhr commented on the cloud of witnesses who helped to shape and strengthen the Niebuhr family members. The strong threads that wove together the Niebuhr family were represented in a variety of textures and colors. Gustav Niebuhr's obituary carried a detailed report of the funeral service. The Reverend F. P. Jens spoke on behalf of the Deaconess

Federation and noted Gustav's "living faith," which would ensure that his work would not die with him.

> He lived in humbleness of heart and his whole life was a living testimonial of how the Grace of God works through sinful men and women....Rev. Niebuhr was fearless and manly in fighting for the right. He spent his days not seeking personal gain and [seeking] the advancement of the kingdom of his Master.[40]

In a section during the funeral for tributes from fellow pastors, the Reverend G. W. Wise, pastor of the First Christian Church, reminded the congregation of the need for effective leadership in the world. "The church has often failed for competent leadership—a man with a vision of what ought to be a wisdom and force of Christian character to convert the vision into reality. All the elements of leadership were happily combined in the life and character of brother Niebuhr."[41]

At the memorial service for Hulda Niebuhr, the dean of McCormick Theological Seminary, Floyd Filson, reminded the community of Hulda's birth as a

> daughter of the manse. In this Christian home she received as a living treasure the heritage of the Gospel. When on April 17, 1959, she came with courage to the end of her vital ministry, she had made that heritage significant to multitudes of children, young people and adults still willing to learn.[42]

Two years later, the McCormick community mourned the death, yet celebrated the life, of Lydia Niebuhr and the contribution she had made to so many lives during her years of ministry. Edward F. Campbell and Phyllis Campbell were among those who represented the McCormick community at Lydia's funeral. At the end of a brief recitation of Lydia's life, Edward Campbell closed with these words:

> Jesus said to his disciples, "Suffer the little children to come unto me, for of such is the kingdom of Heaven." Surely then Lydia Niebuhr had more contact with the kingdom of heaven than anyone else I know. For 91 years she kept young in her faith by what she learned from the children to whom the kingdom belongs. Her example, her life, has reached us all.[43]

Hulda's nephew, Richard R. Niebuhr, was correct in his assumption about family members and the mantles that they pass on to each other. Common in the memorials to Gustav and Lydia and Hulda is a living faith that touched the hearts and lives of those with whom they came in contact. They had a commitment to a vision of God's realm and followed that vision, each in her or his own way.

In a statement that was written in recognition of Hulda's anticipated retirement, Arthur McKay, president of McCormick Seminary, described the marks of a good teacher that Hulda knew and practiced. A good teacher must know her subject, must like her subject, and must have a genuine concern for her students.

> She has been a shining example of the creative and imaginative scholar. Hulda Niebuhr has touched the lives of her students with kindness and generous self-giving.... Her retirement at commencement this year provides the opportunity to honor her for those qualities of heart and mind which her colleagues on the McCormick Theological Seminary faculty and her students have long known and admired, and to express deep appreciation for her as teacher and friend.[44]

Notable in these comments is the phrase, "creative and imaginative scholar." Hulda made her way in the world as a single, professional woman with confidence in her abilities as an educator. She probably knew that she taught differently from others, but she never thought of herself as anything less than a "creative and imaginative scholar." The last academic institution in which she taught and lived was able to appreciate her contribution and to realize that "creative," "intelligent," and "scholar" are not mutually exclusive terms. Rather, they served to describe accurately the remarkable talents she possessed and passed on as a legacy to those who would follow her.

Hulda Niebuhr's life does provide important threads to the understanding of the tapestry of vocational journeys of women. Hulda's journey was one of claiming her voice within her family and within the institutions in which she worked. Though an unmarried professional woman, she was not single. She did have family structures and support that enabled her development as a competent professional woman. Her reluctance as a pioneer does not diminish the contribution she made to our understanding of the developmental and vocational journeys of women who have been our foremothers.

The Writings of Hulda Niebuhr

UNPUBLISHED WORK

This and That, a collection of poems, 1929. Archives, Jesuit-Krauss-McCormick Library, McCormick Theological Seminary, Chicago.

BOOKS

Greatness Passing By: Stories to Tell Boys and Girls. New York: Charles Scribner's Sons, 1931.
Ventures in Dramatics: With Boys and Girls of the Church School. New York: Charles Scribner's Sons, 1935.
With Barbara Keppel-Compton, trans. Fritz Kunkel, *What It Means To Grow Up: A Guide in Understanding the Development of Character*. New York: Charles Scribner's Sons, 1947.
The One Story. Philadelphia: Westminster Press, 1948.

ARTICLES

International Journal of Religious Education
    "Candy and the Kingdom." February 1933:16–17.
    "Thanksgiving for Our Time." November 1933:13–14, 40.
    "Teaching the Bible to Junior Highs through Dramatization." February 1941:9–10.
    "Memorial Service: Keep Them Near Thee." July–August 1944:11–12.
    "Trying on Life." October 1954:12–13, 37.

McCormick Speaking, alumni publication of McCormick Theological Seminary, Archives, Jesuit-Krauss-McCormick Library, McCormick Theological Seminary, Chicago.
    "The Minister's Child." February 1950, 7–10.
    "Dull Teaching is Unbiblical." February 1951, 12–14.
    "Red Roses and Sin." November 1951, 7–10.
    "A Seeming Dilemma in Christian Education." October 1953, 3–7, 15.
    "Are We Raising Nominal Christians?" January 1955, 10–13.
    "Learning By Heart—Then and Now." May 1955, 9–11.
    "Singleness of Heart." November 1955, 3–6.
    "A Testimony." March 1956, 11–12, 15.
    "Is Christian Education True to its Reformation Heritage?" April 1957, 13–15.
    "Communicating the Gospel through Christian Education." March 1958, 13–14.
    "The Teacher's Authority." February 1959, 7–12, 22.

OTHER PUBLISHED ARTICLES

    "Yes and No." *Counsel* 1, no. 1 (October-December 1948): 11–12.
    "Spiritual Progenitors." *The Pulpit* 26, no. 6 (June 1955): 2–4.
    "Know Children as Persons." *Christian Century*, 5 April 1957:423–24.
    "Red Roses and Sin." *The Pulpit*, June 1958:12–13.

Notes

INTRODUCTION

1. Richard R. Niebuhr, "Foreword," in *A Father's Mantle: The Legacy of Gustav Niebuhr*, William G. Chrystal (New York: The Pilgrim Press, 1982), x.
2. Ibid., xi.
3. Eulogy of Hulda Niebuhr, 20 April 1959, Archives, Jesuit-Krauss-McCormick Library, McCormick Theological Seminary, Chicago.
4. Ibid.
5. Helen Haroutunian, interview by author, 1 April 1987.
6. Jane Marcus, "Invisible Mending," in *Between Women*, ed. Carol Ascher, Louise DeSalvo, and Sara Ruddick (Boston: Beacon Press, 1984). Marcus discusses the task of writing history using the metaphor of weaving so that the lives and the work of women can be recovered and rewoven back into the culture's memory or "fabric."

7. Blanche Wiesen Cook, "Biographer and Subject: A Critical Connection," in *Between Women*, ed. Ascher, DeSalvo, Ruddick, 398.

CHAPTER 1

1. In his book *A Father's Mantle: The Legacy of Gustav Niebuhr*, Chrystal notes that this church had been founded in 1854 by immigrants from Lippe-Detmold, the province from which Gustav Niebuhr had come (New York: The Pilgrim Press, 12).
2. Herbert G. Gutman, *Work, Culture and Society in Industrializing America* (New York: Alfred A. Knopf, 1976), 81. Gutman attributes this change to Protestant denominations and their leadership, who chose to "bless and defend" society.
3. Ibid., 83.
4. Frederick Fox, "Our Church in California," *Reformed Church Messenger*, 16 June 1869:4, quoted in Chrystal, *A Father's Mantle,* 31.
5. Gustav Niebuhr, "Kirchliches Bewusstsein," *Der Friedensbote* 52, no. 10 (10 March 1901): 77, quoted in Chrystal, *A Father's Mantle*, 65.
6. I agree with Chrystal in *A Father's Mantle* when he states that these concepts provided the "theological fulcrum" that was the basis for the development of the Niebuhr children's faith and practice (113).
7. Jon Diefenthaler, *H. Richard Niebuhr: A Lifetime of Reflections on the Church and the World* (Macon: Mercer University Press, 1986), x.
8. For more detailed descriptions of the Niebuhrs' home life, see Chrystal, *A Father's Mantle*; Jon Diefenthaler, *H. Richard Niebuhr*; and June Bingham, *Courage to Change: An Introduction to the Life and Thought of Reinhold Niebuhr* (New York: Charles Scribner's Sons, 1961).
9. Chrystal, *A Father's Mantle*, xvi, 112.
10. Ibid., 36.
11. James Fowler, *To See the Kingdom: The Theological Vision of H. Richard Niebuhr* (Nashville: Abingdon Press, 1974), 2.
12. Bingham, *Courage to Change*, 53.
13. Richard Wightman Fox, *Reinhold Niebuhr: A Biography* (New York: Pantheon Books, 1985), 5.
14. Mary Kimbrough, "Associate Pastor Role for Mother," *St. Louis Post-Dispatch*, 23 October 1953.
15. Ibid.
16. William Chrystal, "Interpreters of Our Faith: Gustav Niebuhr," *A.D. Magazine,* July–August 1979:19.

17. Kimbrough, "Associate Pastor."
18. Ibid.
19. Hulda Niebuhr, *Greatness Passing By* (New York: Charles Scribner's Sons, 1931), xiv.
20. Ralph C. Abele, "A Woman Named Lydia," *United Church Herald*, 17 December 1959, 10.
21. Bingham, *Courage to Change*, 53.
22. R. Fox, *Reinhold Niebuhr*, 10–11.
23. Hulda Niebuhr, letter to June Bingham, 5 April 1959, copy in the hands of the author.
24. Bingham, *Courage to Change*, 57.
25. Chrystal, *A Father's Mantle*, 39.
26. Ibid.
27. Ibid.
28. Ibid., 35–36.
29. R. Fox, *Reinhold Niebuhr*, 8. Fox's assumption about Hulda's being a "mirror image of her mother" will be challenged in the last part of this chapter.
30. Nancy Cott, *The Grounding of Modern Feminism* (New Haven: Yale University Press, 1987), 22.
31. Ibid., 16.
32. Ibid.
33. Chrystal, *A Father's Mantle*, 38.
34. Cott, *Grounding*, 37.
35. Ibid., 39.
36. Chrystal, *A Father's Mantle*, 39.
37. Cott, *Grounding*, 17.
38. Ibid.
39. Chrystal, *A Father's Mantle*, 15.
40. John Bodnar, *The Transplanted: A History of Immigrants in Urban America* (Bloomington: Indiana University Press, 1985), 168.
41. David Dunn, Paul N. Crusius, Josias Friedli, Theophil W. Menzel, Carl E. Schneider, William Toth, and James E. Wagner, *A History of the Evangelical and Reformed Church* (Philadelphia: The Christian Education Press, 1961), 197.
42. Ibid., 196.
43. Ibid., 216.
44. Chrystal, *A Father's Mantle*, 47.
45. Ibid., 79.
46. Ibid.

47. Ibid., 80.
48. Ibid., 82.
49. 1904 address at the Ninth Protestant Deaconess Conference in St. Louis, quoted in ibid., 84.
50. Ibid., 90.
51. Ibid., 87.
52. Ibid.
53. Ursula Niebuhr, *Remembering Reinhold Niebuhr: Letters of Reinhold and Ursula M. Niebuhr* (San Francisco: Harper & Row, 1991), 416–17.
54. Chrystal, *A Father's Mantle*, 88.
55. Hulda Niebuhr, letter to Harry Cotton, 16 May 1945, Archives, Jesuit-Krauss-McCormick Library, McCormick Theological Seminary, Chicago.
56. U. Niebuhr, *Remembering Reinhold*, 417.
57. Christopher Niebuhr, letter to author, 27 July 1987.
58. Chrystal, "Interpreters of Our Faith," 19.
59. R. Fox, *Reinhold Niebuhr*, 5.
60. Nancy Chodorow, *The Reproduction of Mothering: Psychoanalysis and the Sociology of Gender* (Berkeley: University of California Press, 1978), 109.
61. Hulda Niebuhr, *This and That*, December 1929, a collection of unpublished poetry, Archives, Jesuit-Krauss-McCormick Library, McCormick Theological Seminary, Chicago.

CHAPTER 2

1. Adele E. Hosto, "Principles and Experiences in Parish Deaconess Work," *Der Evangelische Diakonissen-Herold,* 1916:3.
2. R. Fox, *Reinhold Niebuhr*, 44.
3. Ibid.
4. Anniversary Record, Commemorating the Twenty-Fifth Anniversary of Bethel Evangelical Church, Detroit, Michigan, October 17–31, 1937.
5. Ibid.
6. Ibid.
7. Ibid.
8. Bingham, *Courage to Change*, 104.
9. Florence C. Schulz, letter to John Helt, n.d., copy in the hands of the author.
10. L[ydia] Niebuhr, "Week-Day Activities," *Sunday School Work in the*

Evangelical Synod of North America, 1916–1919: Official Report of the Second National Convocation of Evangelical Sunday Schools, n.p., 131.

11. Ibid.
12. Ibid., 132.
13. Ibid.
14. Ibid.
15. Ibid., 133.
16. Abele, "A Woman Named Lydia," 11.
17. Ursula Niebuhr, letter to author, 2 September 1987.
18. H. Niebuhr, *This and That.*
19. Chodorow, *The Reproduction of Mothering,* 36. Chodorow uses the term "reproduce" to describe the way that women take care of their families physically, psychologically, and maternally. She suggests that in terms of their own support and reconstitution both emotionally and affectively within the family, no one reproduces them.
20. Carl Degler, *At Odds: Women and the Family in America from the Revolution to the Present* (Oxford: Oxford University Press, 1980), 413.
21. Ibid., 164.
22. Ibid., 148.
23. Ibid., 191.
24. Ibid., 415.
25. Charles McIver, *New York City Tribune,* 28 January 1861, quoted in ibid., 314.
26. R. Fox, *Reinhold Niebuhr,* 39. Fox indicates that Walter's ventures into newspaper management had crushed him both financially and personally and that Reinhold was looked upon to provide the male leadership in the family.
27. Obituary, Walter Scott Athearn, *The Christian Student,* Nov. 1934:28 (Special Collections, Mugar Library, Boston University, Boston).
28. H. Niebuhr, "So Much To Do," in *This and That.*
29. Boston University Year Book, 1922–25, 500.
30. Hulda's transcript from the University of Chicago indicates that her major at Lincoln College was home economics. Her home address was listed as 535 N. Union Street, Lincoln, Illinois. This leads to the question of why she listed as home a place she had not lived in for six years. Her transcript at Boston University listed her home as 2726 Lothrop Avenue, Detroit, Michigan.
31. H. Niebuhr, letter to Harry Cotton, 16 May 1945.

32. Ibid.
33. Boston University Year Book, 1922–25, 499.
34. Ibid., 473.
35. Ibid., 474.
36. Hulda Niebuhr, "Children's Lies: A Psychological Study with Special Reference to German Source Material," Master's thesis, Boston University, 1927.
37. H. Niebuhr, letter to Harry Cotton, 16 May 1945.
38. H. Niebuhr, "And He Stood Over Her," in *This and That.*
39. H. Niebuhr, "The Train" (6 March 1924), in *This and That.*
40. Ibid.
41. Ibid.
42. Hulda Niebuhr, *Ventures in Dramatics* (New York: Charles Scribner's Sons, 1935), v.
43. George Albert Coe and Sophia Fahs, faculty members at Union Theological Seminary, were leaders in the field of religious education who worked to integrate educational methodology and a liberal theological approach to religious education.
44. Alberta Munkres, *Which Way for Our Children?* (New York: Charles Scribner's Sons, 1936), 77.
45. *To Phos,* 1925, Special Collections, Mugar Library, Boston University, Boston, 17.
46. H. Niebuhr, "My Daddy Can Fix It!" in *This and That.*
47. H. Niebuhr, "Titles," in *This and That.*
48. R. Fox, *Reinhold Niebuhr*, 90.
49. H. Niebuhr, *This and That.*
50. Ibid.
51. Schulz, letter to John Helt, n.d.
52. H. Niebuhr, *Greatness Passing By*, xii.
53. Ibid., xiii.
54. H. Niebuhr, "What Some of Them Said," in *This and That.*

CHAPTER 3

1. Hulda Niebuhr, letter to Harry Cotton, 2 March 1945, Archives, Jesuit-Krauss-McCormick Library, McCormick Theological Seminary, Chicago.
2. Ibid.
3. Boston University Bulletin, 1928–1930, Special Collections, Mugar Library, Boston University, Boston, 667.
4. R. Fox, *Reinhold Niebuhr*, 106.

5. Ibid.
6. Ibid., 50.
7. Ibid., 118. Evidently this depression and sense of abandonment either did not exist or did not last for a long period of time since Lydia was able to quickly establish new roots and commitments with the Madison Avenue Presbyterian Church where her daughter was employed.
8. Ibid., 131.
9. The transcript of her last quarter of study indicates three courses taken (one at Union and two at Teacher's College) with no grades reported. Of the two courses at Teacher's College, one indicates an incomplete and the other an absence from the final exam.
10. Union Theological Seminary Annual Catalog, Part 1, 1930–1931, Library, Union Theological Seminary, New York, 47–48.
11. H. Niebuhr, "Rap-a-Tap!" in *This and That.*
12. Eleanor Slater, letter to Hulda Niebuhr, n.d., Archives, Jesuit-Krauss-McCormick Library, McCormick Theological Seminary, Chicago.
13. Carol Buchanan, interview by author, 31 August 1989.
14. R. Fox, *Reinhold Niebuhr,* 121. Fox provides the documentation on this correspondence. Any evidence of this conversation between H. Richard Niebuhr and Hulda Niebuhr has been lost since H. Richard destroyed their correspondence upon her death.
15. Ibid.
16. U. Niebuhr, *Remembering Reinhold,* 417.
17. H. Niebuhr, letter to Harry Cotton, 2 March 1945.
18. See Lawrence A. Cremin, "Scientists, Sentimentalists and Radicals," in *The Transformation of the School* (New York: Vintage Books, 1961), 215–21. Cremin discusses the difference in focus between Kilpatrick and Dewey. Kilpatrick shifted the focus from curriculum to the child, a position that Cremin believes Dewey later rejected.
19. Dorothy Jean Furnish, "Sophia Lyon Fahs" (Paper presented at the annual meeting of the History Task Force of the Association of Professors and Researchers in Religious Education, New York, N. Y., 4 November 1989), 2.
20. *The Weekly,* 9 September 1930, Archives, Madison Avenue Presbyterian Church, New York.
21. Ibid.
22. "Miss Niebuhr Resigns," *The Madison Avenue Presbyterian Church News,* 4 May 1945, 3.
23. H. Niebuhr, letter to Harry Cotton, 2 March 1945.

24. *The Weekly*, 9 September 1930.
25. Fox, *Reinhold Niebuhr*, 118. Fox attributes Lydia's depression and despondency to the end of her role as Reinhold's parish associate in Detroit. Fox fails to take account of Lydia's quick attachment to Madison Avenue Presbyterian Church, which would soon lead to a new partnership in ministry with her daughter.
26. H. Niebuhr, letter to Harry Cotton, 2 March 1945.
27. These articles can be found in *The Weekly* and its successor, *Madison Avenue Presbyterian Church News,* 1930–1945, Archives, Madison Avenue Presbyterian Church, New York.
28. George Buttrick, "The History of the Madison Avenue Presbyterian Church," *Madison Avenue Presbyterian Church News,* 5 May 1939, 4.
29. 150th Anniversary Celebration booklet, Madison Avenue Presbyterian Church, New York, New York, Fall 1984.
30. Ibid.
31. Ibid.
32. Buttrick, "History of Madison Avenue Church," 4.
33. H. Niebuhr, letter to Harry Cotton, 2 March 1945.
34. "This Is Our Church," *Madison Avenue Presbyterian Church News,* 2 June 1944, 5.
35. Buttrick, "History of Madison Avenue Church," 6.
36. Ibid.
37. Ibid., 7.
38. Ibid.
39. "Who's Who?" *The Weekly,* Madison Avenue Presbyterian Church, 4 December 1936, 7.
40. Ibid.
41. Hulda Niebuhr, letter to Ted Braun, 3 February 1959, Archives, Jesuit-Krauss-McCormick Library, McCormick Theological Seminary, Chicago.
42. Ibid.
43. *The Weekly,* Madison Avenue Presbyterian Church, 9 October 1931, 3.
44. "Lenten School for Adults—1944," *Madison Avenue Presbyterian Church News,* 18 February 1944, 3.
45. *Madison Avenue Presbyterian Church News,* 5 January 1945, 3.
46. Ibid., 22 December 1939, 3.
47. Ibid., 31 March 1941, 1.
48. H. Niebuhr, *Greatness Passing By*, xv.

49. Ibid., xii.
50. Ibid., xvii.
51. Ibid., xix.
52. Advertisement for *Greatness Passing By*, in *Religious Education* 26, nos. 5–6 (May–June 1931): 491.
53. H. Niebuhr, *Ventures in Dramatics*, xv.
54. Ibid., xiii.
55. Review of *Ventures in Dramatics*, by Hulda Niebuhr, *Religious Education* 31, no. 1 (October 1936): 76.
56. Hulda Niebuhr, "Teaching the Bible to Junior Highs through Dramatization," *International Journal of Religious Education* 17, no. 6 (February 1941): 10.
57. Ibid.
58. Hulda Niebuhr, "Keep Them Near Thee," *International Journal of Religious Education* 20, no. 11 (July–August 1944): 12.
59. Hulda Niebuhr, letter to Harry Cotton, 16 May 1945, Archives, Jesuit-Krauss-McCormick Library, McCormick Theological Seminary, Chicago.
60. D. Campbell Wyckoff, letter to author, 31 March 1990.
61. Ibid.
62. *Madison Avenue Presbyterian Church News,* 16 May 1941, 2.
63. Ibid.
64. Hulda Niebuhr, "Candy and the Kingdom," *International Journal of Religious Education* 9, no. 6 (February 1933): 16.
65. Ibid., 17.
66. Hulda Niebuhr, "Communicating the Gospel Through Christian Education," *McCormick Speaking* 11, no. 6 (1958): 13.
67. Ibid., 15.
68. "Miss Niebuhr Speaks to Teachers," *Madison Avenue Presbyterian Church News* 7, no. 19 (11 May 1945): 1.
69. Ibid.
70. *Madison Avenue Presbyterian Church News* 7, no. 18 (4 May 1945): 3.

CHAPTER 4

1. Jananne L. Thompson, letter to Joan Beebe, 1 February 1979, copy in the hands of the author.
2. H. Niebuhr, letter to Harry Cotton, 2 March 1945.
3. Ibid.

4. Hulda Niebuhr, letter to Harry Cotton, 11 December 1945, Archives, Jesuit-Krauss-McCormick Library, McCormick Theological Seminary, Chicago.
5. Ibid.
6. Ibid.
7. Harry Cotton, letter to Hulda Niebuhr, 27 February 1945, Archives, Jesuit-Krauss-McCormick Library, McCormick Theological Seminary, Chicago.
8. Annual Report of the Presbyterian College of Christian Education to the Presbytery of Chicago, 6 March 1944, Archives, Jesuit-Krauss-McCormick Library, McCormick Theological Seminary, Chicago, 2.
9. H. Niebuhr, letter to Harry Cotton, 11 December 1945.
10. H. Niebuhr, letter to Harry Cotton, 2 March 1945.
11. "Announcement of Teachers College, 1945–46," Teachers College, Columbia University, New York, 80.
12. Ibid., 81.
13. H. Niebuhr, letter to Harry Cotton, 16 May 1945.
14. H. Niebuhr, letter to Harry Cotton, 1945, Archives, Jesuit-Krauss-McCormick Library, McCormick Theological Seminary, Chicago.
15. H. Niebuhr, letter to Harry Cotton, 29 January 1946.
16. H. Niebuhr, letter to Harry Cotton, 11 December 1945.
17. Ibid.
18. Hulda Niebuhr, letter to Harry Cotton, 13 December 1945, Archives, Jesuit-Krauss-McCormick Library, McCormick Theological Seminary, Chicago.
19. H. Niebuhr, letter to Harry Cotton, 18 December 1945.
20. Harry Cotton, letter to Hulda Niebuhr, 26 December 1945, Archives, Jesuit-Krauss-McCormick Library, McCormick Theological Seminary, Chicago.
21. H. Niebuhr, letter to Harry Cotton, 2 January 1946, Archives, Jesuit-Krauss-McCormick Library, McCormick Theological Seminary, Chicago.
22. H. Niebuhr, letter to Harry Cotton, 1945.
23. Harry Cotton, letter to Hulda Niebuhr, 27 July 1945, Archives, Jesuit-Krauss-McCormick Library, McCormick Theological Seminary, Chicago.
24. H. Niebuhr, letter to Harry Cotton, 2 March 1945.
25. H. Niebuhr, letter to Harry Cotton, 16 May 1945.
26. H. Niebuhr, letter to Harry Cotton, 11 December 1945.
27. H. Niebuhr, letter to Harry Cotton, 18 December 1945.

28. Ibid.
29. Ibid.
30. H. Niebuhr, letter to Harry Cotton, 29 January 1946.
31. H. Niebuhr, letter to Harry Cotton, 2 January 1946.
32. Mary Duckert, "Interpreters of Our Faith: Hulda Niebuhr," *A.D. Magazine,* September 1976:36.
33. Ronald H. Stone, *Reinhold Niebuhr: Prophet to Politicians* (Nashville: Abingdon Press, 1974), 19.
34. Hulda Niebuhr, "Spiritual Progenitors," *The Pulpit* 266 (June 1955): 3.
35. Ibid.
36. Ibid.
37. Ibid.
38. Ibid., 4.
39. Hulda Niebuhr, "Are We Raising Nominal Christians?" *McCormick Speaking* 9, no. 6 (1956): 13.
40. Paul Krebill, letter to author, 13 April 1988.
41. Norman D. Nettleton, letter to author, 28 December 1987.
42. Georgie Frame Madison, letter to author, 4 April 1988.
43. Mary Duckert, interview by author, 22 April 1987.
44. Robert Worley, interview by author, 29 April 1987.
45. Nettleton, letter to author, 28 December 1987.
46. Hulda Niebuhr, "Know Children as Persons," *The Christian Century,* 3 April 1947:423.
47. Ibid.
48. Rev. June K. Stansbery, letter to author, 5 April 1988.
49. Ibid.
50. Hulda Niebuhr, "Junior Sermon," in *Twentieth Century Encyclopedia of Religious Knowledge* (Grand Rapids: Baker Book House, 1955), 620.
51. Hulda Niebuhr, "Red Roses and Sin," *The Pulpit,* June 1958:13.
52. Ibid.
53. Ibid, 12.
54. Hulda Niebuhr, "Yes and No," *Counsel* 1, no. 1 (October–December 1948): 12.
55. Ibid.
56. H. Niebuhr, "Teaching the Bible through Dramatization," 10.
57. Nada M. Barnett, letter to author, 29 January 1988.
58. Madison, letter to author, 4 April 1988.
59. H. Niebuhr, *Greatness Passing By,* xi, xii.
60. Barnett, letter to author, 29 January 1988.

61. Krebill, letter to author, 13 April 1988.
62. Madison, letter to author, 4 April 1988.
63. Worley, interview by author, 29 April 1987.
64. Hulda Niebuhr, "A Seeming Dilemma in Christian Education," *McCormick Speaking* 7, no.1 (1953): 6.
65. Ibid., 3.
66. Hulda Niebuhr, "Is Christian Education True to its Reformation Heritage?" *McCormick Speaking* 10, no. 8 (1957): 15.
67. H. Niebuhr, "A Seeming Dilemma in Christian Education," 7.
68. Hulda Niebuhr, "Learning by Heart—Then and Now," *McCormick Speaking* 8, no. 8 (1955): 11.
69. Barnett, letter to author, 29 January 1988. One of Hulda's students, Nada M. Barnett, interpreted Hulda's use of "warp and woof" to mean the "whole fabric of our faith." The other expression that she remembered from class was "pooling of ignorances," which Hulda used to remind her students that discussions in class were to be more than that.
70. Richard E. Wylie, letter to author, 6 January 1988.
71. A. Wayne Benson, letter to author, 20 February 1988.
72. Mary Duckert, "Interpreters of Our Faith: Hulda Niebuhr," *A.D. Magazine*, September 1976, 36.
73. Inauguration Bulletin, 13 January 1953, Archives, Jesuit-Krauss-McCormick Library, McCormick Theological Seminary, Chicago.
74. H. Niebuhr, letter to Harry Cotton, n.d., Archives, Jesuit-Krauss-McCormick Library, McCormick Theological Seminary, Chicago.
75. Ibid.
76. Wylie, letter to author, 6 January 1988.
77. Oscar Hussel, letter to Joan Beebe, 20 December 1978, copy in the hands of the author.
78. Mary Duckert, letter to Joan Beebe, 16 January 1979, copy in the hands of the author.
79. Mary Duckert, "Interpreters of Our Faith," 36.
80. Beatrice M. Mills, letter to Joan Beebe, 24 January 1979, copy in the hands of the author.
81. Duckert, letter to Joan Beebe, 16 January 1979.
82. Ibid.
83. H. Niebuhr, letter to Ted Braun, 3 February 1959.
84. Ibid.
85. Abele, "A Woman Named Lydia," 5.
86. H. Niebuhr, letter to Ted Braun, 3 February 1959.
87. "It'll Be Mrs. Niebuhr's Day," *Chicago Daily News*, 29 May 1959.

88. Rev. June K. Stansbery, letter to Joan Beebe, 12 March 1979, copy in the hands of the author.
89. Hulda Niebuhr, letter to Worth Frank, n.d., Archives, Jesuit-Krauss-McCormick Library, McCormick Theological Seminary, Chicago.
90. Arthur McKay, letter to Hulda Niebuhr, 10 January 1959, Archives, Jesuit-Krauss-McCormick Library, McCormick Theological Seminary, Chicago.
91. Hulda Niebuhr, letter to Arthur McKay, 19 January 1959, Archives, Jesuit-Krauss-McCormick Library, McCormick Theological Seminary, Chicago.
92. Arthur McKay, letter to Hulda Niebuhr, 23 January 1959, Archives, Jesuit-Krauss-McCormick Library, McCormick Theological Seminary, Chicago.
93. Arthur McKay, letter to Reinhold Niebuhr, 30 April 1959, Archives, Jesuit-Krauss-McCormick Library, McCormick Theological Seminary, Chicago.
94. Reinhold Niebuhr, letter to Arthur McKay, 20 April 1959, Archives, Jesuit-Krauss-McCormick Library, McCormick Theological Seminary, Chicago.
95. H. Richard Niebuhr, letter to Arthur McKay, 5 February 1961, Archives, Jesuit-Krauss-McCormick Library, McCormick Theological Seminary, Chicago.
96. Ibid.
97. Arthur McKay, letter to H. Richard Niebuhr, 3 April 1962, Archives, Jesuit-Krauss-McCormick Library, McCormick Theological Seminary, Chicago.

CHAPTER 5

1. Chrystal, *A Father's Mantle*, 38.
2. Ibid.
3. Ibid., 39.
4. Oscar Hussel, letter to Joan Beebe, 20 December 1978, copy in the hands of the author.
5. Rosalind Rosenberg, *Beyond Separate Spheres: Intellectual Roots of Modern Feminism* (New Haven: Yale University Press, 1982), xii.
6. Ibid., xv.
7. Ibid., 43.
8. Ibid., 47. As dean at the University of Chicago in 1892, Talbot fought for equality for women. Rosenberg refers to her as a leader in the "feminization of academe."

9. Ibid., 239.
10. Ibid., 27.
11. Orvid R. Sellers, *The Fifth Quarter Century of McCormick: The Story of the Years 1929-1954 at McCormick Theological Seminary* (Chicago: McCormick Theological Seminary, 1955), 96.
12. Hussel, letter to Joan Beebe, 20 December 1978.
13. Luella Cotton, letter to author, 15 September 1987.
14. Hulda Niebuhr, *The One Story* (Philadelphia: Westminster Press, 1949), 12.
15. Madeleine R. Grumet, *Bitter Milk: Women and Teaching* (Amherst: University of Massachusetts Press, 1988), 191.
16. Ibid., 58.
17. H. Niebuhr, "Communicating the Gospel," 13.
18. H. Niebuhr, "Red Roses and Sin," 13.
19. Ibid.
20. H. Niebuhr, "Communicating the Gospel," 15.
21. Hulda Niebuhr, "Thanksgiving for Our Time," *International Journal of Religious Education* 10, no. 3 (1933): 13.
22. Hulda Niebuhr, "The Teacher's Authority," *McCormick Speaking* 12, no. 3 (1959): 8.
23. Hulda Niebuhr, "Is Christian Education True to Its Reformation Heritage?" *McCormick Speaking* 10, no. 8 (1957): 15.
24. H. Niebuhr, "The Teacher's Authority," 12.
25. H. Niebuhr, "Learning by Heart," 11.
26. Hulda Niebuhr, "Singleness of Heart," *McCormick Speaking* 9, no. 3 (1955): 50.
27. H. Niebuhr, "Teaching the Bible through Dramatization," 10.
28. Hulda Niebuhr, "Are We Raising Nominal Christians?" *McCormick Speaking* 8, no. 4 (1955): 12.
29. Mary Field Belenky, Blythe McVicker Clinchy, Nancy Rule Goldberger, and Jill Mattuck Tarule, *Women's Ways of Knowing: The Development of Self, Voice, and Mind* (New York: Basic Books, 1986), 193. Belenky et al. discovered in their interviews with women that essential for those women was having confidence in their own intellectual abilities and gaining it an an early age. Hulda seems to have exhibited that quality.
30. Ibid., 194. Belenky et al. contrast the ongoing process of confirmation with the masculine myth that affirms confirmation as the result or culmination of the educational process. Such an understanding of education as continued development seems to affirm a praxis methodology, acknowledging the importance of a cyclical model of dialog,

action, and reflection. Hulda's life would affirm their assumption that in the course of female development, confirmation and community precede and are necessary qualities for development, not the result.

31. Association of Professors and Researchers in Religious Education, annual meeting of the History Task Force, New York, N.Y., 3 November 1989.

32. Sara Ruddick, "Maternal Thinking," *Feminist Studies* 6, no. 2 (1980): 342–67. Ruddick describes a maternal thinker as one concerned with preservation of the learner, enabling her growth and nurturing her movement into the world.

33. Hussel, letter to Joan Beebe, 20 December 1978.

34. Stansbery, letter to Joan Beebe, 12 March 1979.

35. Duckert, "Interpreters of Our Faith," 36.

36. "Professor Hulda Niebuhr: In Appreciation," Memorial Service, 20 April 1959, Archives, Jesuit-Krauss-McCormick Library, McCormick Theological Seminary, Chicago.

37. W. Douglas Sampson, letter to author, April 1987.

38. Rosalie W. Mixon, letter to author, April 1987.

39. Sampson, letter to author, April 1987.

40. "Last Rites for Rev. Niebuhr," *Lincoln Daily News-Herald,* 23 April 1913.

41. Ibid.

42. "Professor Hulda Niebuhr: In Appreciation."

43. "Lydia Niebuhr," Eulogy, 27(?) January 1961, Archives, Jesuit-Krauss-McCormick Library, McCormick Theological Seminary, Chicago, Illinois.

44. Arthur R. McKay, "Hulda Niebuhr as Teacher," *McCormick Speaking* 12, no. 4 (1959): 20.